God Cares,
But Do We?

God Cares, But Do We?
Copyright © 2022 by Kwaku Adjei Mensah

Published in the United States of America

ISBN   Paperback: 978-1-959761-19-8
ISBN   eBook: 978-1-959761-20-4

All rights reserved. No part of this publication may be reproduced, stored in a retrieval system or transmitted in any way by any means, electronic, mechanical, photocopy, recording or otherwise without the prior permission of the author except as provided by USA copyright law.

The opinions expressed by the author are not necessarily those of ReadersMagnet, LLC.

ReadersMagnet, LLC
10620 Treena Street, Suite 230 | San Diego, California, 92131 USA
1.619. 354. 2643 | www.readersmagnet.com

Book design copyright © 2022 by ReadersMagnet, LLC. All rights reserved.

Cover design by Kent Gabutin
Layout design by Daniel Lopez

God Cares, But Do We?

The Evolution of Belief and Spirituality

Kwaku Adjei Mensah

ReadersMagnet, LLC

To God, with whom all things are possible, who I believe has given me this gift and the words to write
To Ralph and Kay Mensah, my father and mother, who I love with all my heart and have been a blessing to me throughout my life journey, which has made this book possible. Thank you for everything and being strong to help me reach this point in my life.
To my lovely daughter, Amber, who did the
Drawing page illustration and is very talented.
I'm very proud of her drive and achievements.
Love you always, you will always be my little chocolate Princess!
Your padre!

Acknowledgements

I thank my Creator for the gift he has given me, and I thank him for the sacrifice he has made, allowing his son to live among us to show and lead the way, and I pray that the way may be shown to you as well and may you also be blessed on your journey as I have been.

May your mind and heart be open to everything wonderful in this beautiful world we live in.

Be blessed and prosperous and thank you. And I hope it reaches, teaches and opens the eyes of as many as possible.

Thank you

Introduction

As I begin again anew and come to you to say pay attention! In these last days, to those who will believe as I do, it is through watching the signs of the times and the wicked ways of mankind as the days seem to fly by in the blinking of an eye. You would ask why we die when I see through these eyes and surmise the damage being done under the sun and moon. I for one, praise our Father in heaven and thank him for the sevens embedded in my mind, body, and soul so marked and sealed till the end of time itself as I roll through these streets and this life, asking him for forgiveness for the things I have done, accepting his son as my Lord and Savior always while watching my own ways and actions. So, as I write these words to tell you what it is you do, as I see you and ask you currently. As war rages and you turn the pages of my book and look within yourself and see the misery, we cause with our actions toward each other no matter the color of skin, breed, or creed. The things that we do to each other who are made in his image. What right have any of you to take a life which he has given us entrusted with such a blessing a lesson to be learned. I for one am trying my best to pay heed to the Ten Commandments that he has given us to follow not just Hollow words said out of one's mouth. I ask you, what is wrong with what has been written in stone to follow? I list them now as follows:

- I am the lord thy God, which have brought thee out of the land of Egypt, out of the house of bondage. Thou shalt have no other gods before Me.
- Thou shalt not make unto thee any graven image, or any likeness of anything that is in heaven above, or that is in the earth beneath, or that is in the water under the earth. Thou shalt not bow down thyself to them, nor serve them: for I the lord thy God am a jealous God, visiting the iniquity of the fathers upon the children unto the third and fourth generation of them that hate me; and showing mercy unto thousands of them that love me, and keep my commandments.
- Thou shalt not take the name of the lord thy God in vain; for the lord will not hold him guiltless that taketh his name in vain.
- Remember the Sabbath day, to keep it holy. Six days shalt thou labor, and do all thy work: But the seventh day is the Sabbath of the lord thy God: in it thou shalt not do any work, thou, nor thy son, nor thy daughter, thy manservant, nor thy maidservant, nor thy cattle, nor thy stranger that is within thy gates: For in six days the lord made heaven and earth, the sea, and all that in them is, and rested the seventh day: wherefore the lord blessed the Sabbath day, and hallowed it.
- Honor thy father and thy mother: that thy days may be long upon the land which the lord thy God giveth thee.
- Thou shalt not kill.
- Thou shalt not commit adultery.
- Thou shalt not steal.
- Thou shalt not bear false witness against thy neighbor.

- Thou shalt not covet thy neighbor's house; thou shalt not covet thy neighbor's wife, nor his manservant, nor his maidservant, nor his ox, nor his ass, nor any thing that is thy neighbor's.

So, what is wrong with these commandments? Please tell me. I bet you cannot find anything wrong with these basic laws to follow for decent living, respect, honor, and values.

While you remove these things, you wonder why we die or why the world is the way it is today. Since the beginning, Adam and Eve believe as he has said to not eat from the tree, for once the apple was bitten and they were deceived, we have done everything possible to kill ourselves and each other. So, I ask you why you ask why when we lie, deceive, and treat each other so. As I continue through this life and these days, seeing the lack of morals and values, I see the misery we cause each other, no matter the color. I am not perfect and do not claim to be, but I do know I try my best to treat people

> *as I wish to be treated, but in return, what have I gotten in most part? Rotten to the core Lies and manipulations that in the end are your own undoing not mine. I have been used, abused by most, and I do not condemn or bitch or moan, but as I have grown and opened my eyes and have gotten older ever bolder it will not continue, I'm losing my filter slowly, I tell you now in this book and henceforth at times, I may look crazy or whatever, but I have not hurt anyone of you. So, I say to you, what are you looking at? It's not a game. Is there a problem what it is? As you look me up and down walking the streets, I see you… do you really see me? If so then you would not continue your games. And now, as I move on to other matters, I am releasing my stress and addressing issues and things I see around me. I give respect as I say respect is given until you give me a reason*

not to respect you. Some say it is earned. I say everyone is due respect until given a reason not to be respected why should I earn respect from you if you don't earn it from me? Then what does it take to earn respect there are degrees to everything so I give respect due to the fact of you being Gods creation but when you show that you don't respect the fact that I am truly of his creation then in kind you will receive your due. I also say that I would prefer love rather than fear because if you truly love me, then you would see no harm come to me, but if you fear me, then there is no telling what you would do behind my back or in front of my face. I have love for all, no matter the color, race, or breed, but understand that I don't fear you either. You would not want me to fear you because I might then react in a way not appropriate. You do not have any right to take the gift of life our Father has given me. If you think to try, I will defend myself to any degree for I am free of your bondage your chains mentally I am free… physically soon to come you try me and will pay I pray the day never comes but this continuous test continuous manipulations tire me. Now to other matters. Once again, understand where I am coming from. I give praise to our Creator, our Father in heaven, and my Savior, and thank him for his mercy, love, and blessings. My station, our station, to be caretakers of creation and not destroyers. Now let us begin. This is just the beginning of many more to come as I live and breathe poems, writings, music, and whatever he may bless me with.

Not only have you been given these Ten Commandments, which are about honor, trust, and respect, which should not be an issue because we all deserve these. If you expect it should, you will not give it to another that deserves the same. You also have the 42 Laws of MAAT which may or may not be the Ten Commandments Condensed yet still Reasonable Laws or ways for one or society to reach true peace or utopia but so hard for many.

- I have not committed sin.
- I have not committed robbery with violence.
- I have not stolen.
- I have not slain men or women.
- I have not stolen food.
- I have not swindled offerings.
- I have not stolen from God/Goddess.
- I have not told lies.
- I have not carried away food.
- I have not cursed.
- I have not closed my ears to truth.
- I have not committed adultery.
- I have not made anyone cry.
- I have not felt sorrow without reason.
- I have not assaulted anyone.
- I am not deceitful.
- I have not stolen anyone's land.
- I have not been an eavesdropper.
- I have not falsely accused anyone.
- I have not been angry without reason.
- I have not seduced anyone's wife.
- I have not polluted myself.
- I have not terrorized anyone.
- I have not disobeyed the Law.
- I have not been exclusively angry.
- I have not cursed God/Goddess.
- I have not behaved with violence.
- I have not caused disruption of peace.
- I have not acted hastily or without thought.
- I have not overstepped my boundaries of concern.
- I have not exaggerated my words when speaking.

- I have not worked evil.
- I have not used evil thoughts, words or deeds.
- I have not polluted the water.
- I have not spoken angrily or arrogantly.
- I have not cursed anyone in thought, word or deeds.
- I have not placed myself on a pedestal.
- I have not stolen what belongs to God/Goddess.
- I have not stolen from or disrespected the deceased.
- I have not taken food from a child.
- I have not acted with insolence.
- I have not destroyed property belonging to God/ Goddess

The 42 Law of Matt are not bad rules to live by either! It is all about respect and honor for each other and our Creator. If you cannot abide by these simple guidelines of respect for you yourself or others, what do you expect to happen? Order? In this world of chaos? Really? Seriously?

My Feelings Growing Inside Me

As I speak out of this feeling growing inside of me, so many try to doubt cause confusion and disillusion me, but there will be no intrusion no confusion for it is not a game it's not a façade. I give praise to the Most High, our Creator and my Savior, as I mind my behavior. They say the proof is in the pudding and truth in one's actions so as my life my actions even though far from perfect I have given respect, so as I watch the signs of the times and see what I see and believe what I believe, I will not be deceived as I have received the holy spirit and his gift and praise him above all this mess, and thank him that I am blessed by him, yet stressed as I wise up and rise up out of the ashes like a phoenix to be reborn. I have turned my cheek week after week on the innuendos and slights. Not an entertainer or dancer you want answers to questions. I have some answers and questions of my own, but as I write these words that need to be heard, I am gifted in more ways than one. As I give praise to our Father in heaven and Savior.

At times I may act wild and look crazy, but still, I am kind and loving despite adversities, hurdles, and pitfalls as well as overcoming the lies the games and manipulations.

Not a false cause so many are playing and acting on both sides of the fence never been dense but tense now tired of the trickery and slippery actions of snakes. As I look for my Queen

While living this life. Take a walk with me to see that things have grown out of hand, and I begin to land blow after blow and you reap what you sow so as I am king and I bring to bear this gift he has given me, to escape the misery and achieve victory not at all cost for there are prices to be paid, when one plays life as if a game taking for granted the gift that it truly is. Imagine if you will to never have been born to breathe and be alive. As I hear the screams and agony of many and wish to lend a hand, and to take a stand against the atrocities I see being committed, I ask you what is it you do to your fellowman you say mankind but where is the kind in man?

As I speak out not only to you, who are made in his image, but to nature and creation, which our station and position is to be caretakers not destroyers causing destruction which seems to be the only function we are doing now. Acting like a virus upon the world we live consuming everything in our path. Wake up to what is going on around you as I begin to lay down line after line word after word, tearing down the lies as I try to reach out to each and every one. Time is running out as you doubt the truth of things written and consort with your own demise, so be mindful of what you do to each other that are related and created in his image no matter the color, race, or breed in these last days, while watching the wicked ways of mankind I find I am seeing more crazy and deranged actions as the sands of time quicken towards the final hour as I arranged my own affairs; you dare as I care more than you can imagine, but it is not a game, not a joke, so by these keystrokes, I explain this mess you cause with your games your lies the facades that are used that are not the true you, who is to blame is a question asked so many times look in the mirror as things grow clearer there can be no misconception no deception as to the reception that has been received. As I begin to see clearer and grow older and wiser, hoping my warm heart does not get colder by the games of using and abusing each other that is played. then have the nerve to ask why the world is in such a state of dismay. Let's be real as I deal out these blows and grow. The jealousy and envious ways are crazy. Again, I say I know I am not perfect by far, but I know what I am seeing.

There is no surprise to the demise as I make my entry and gently say the lies being told to hold power over others is sickening as nation after nation rise and fall. We are all caught in a melting pot, so hot that it is boiling to the brim as the seasons mix together not of the norm. A storm is brewing on the horizon not surprising while screwing up creation and our station to be caretakers, not destroyers, and so many claiming to be gods with fraudulent actions claiming to be grown but sown nothing but deceit and despair. All I see children doing tit for tat, the killing of innocent men, women, children for nothing more than greed, while wasting precious time and lives in this life as we thrive to survive in Salem's lot watching the world grow hotter and we stand on the edge and the plot thickens as I have my own faults, but as we continue down this road of destruction, we are at the point of breaking or making. What road will we be taking as I make my way through this maze and give praise to our Creator and Savior that a new age is dawning as I yawn and stretch. This life we live is not a game as many claim it to be but a blessing and a lesson to be learned, so I ask, will you burn or learn and earn your way out of this mess as games are played out and time is of the essence?

So, as I watch and say a thing or two about what is going on in the world today with your laws and governments acting like little boys with toys of mass destruction. All the posturing and posing, threatening to destroy each other instead of working together to understand this world we live in and make it a better place for everyone. Instead of making war and weapons of mass destruction how about using all the brilliant minds to make life easier and more pleasant. Longevity of life instead of misery and despair as history should be a lesson learned to avoid past mistakes while exploring every facet of this wondrous world, we live in. Begin to reach out to the stars once we understand where we live and who we are in this place called life.

We were meant for so much more than war and savagery the ugliest facet of humanity its insanity in wanting to wage war on its own world because of ignorant views of few who think they are better because of color. Ones actions combined with words show your value and truth of what you represent in this world, I see where we live and breathe the need ignored because of greed in this world there would be no famine no hunger or homelessness on this bountiful earth that is being plundered for the desires of power over another those that suffer the ones who are the true backbone of society not the few who are chosen by dubious means or lies told of the tip of their tongue. Again, I say, since the dawn of man and Adam and Eve being deceived, we do everything to kill ourselves and each other with the knowledge we have gained the stain being done on this creation like a virus consuming with no concern for the host as mankind ravages its home world not for need but greed. If we continue down this road, then we are headed for certain doom and destruction with the construction of mass weapons, but we can change if we decide to do so, but no we continue to posture to flex and select to destroy not create. Now is the time to make a U-turn and learn not to burn and earn the wings to fly as we try AI and other means to new heights and destinies untold while the wheel of time slowly unfolds the destiny we are choosing.

As I open my eyes to the things around me and surmise the damage and the waste being done, we are yet still factions and fractions of what we should could become in this life. If we make a change in enough time, we can avoid certain doom. I ask you, what will it be? As I watch the unfolding before my very eyes Will we escape or make haste to certain destruction in these last days? As I believe we could and should be so much more if we pull away from this senseless violence and ignorance, we do to each other, every nation, and every race. We chase certain destruction with this air of superiority because of race or breed doing deeds in the name of race purity or cleansing for God? We all are one no matter the color or race. We bleed the same; feel the same pain, sorrow, love, and humiliation. Are we civilized or brutes, I ask you, animal or human? You claim to be mankind but where is the kind in man? It is appalling and disgusting the things I am hearing, see being done all over, and I ask how long will this continue, how long will this be tolerated—this waste of life and this treatment of each other and nature? Seriously, grow up and wake up to the nonsense.

Because it's really sickening, and while he is watching his creation being destroyed by his children and not happy at all since the fall.

I am certain of this whether you believe it or not.

This hell is getting hot, and I myself am done with the games, the lies before my very eyes. as I look for my Queen because I am king and done with the posing. So, as I begin anew, and I tell you once again to watch your step and your mouth because I am beginning to cut short all the games and lies, I am not a killer, not a gangster, but I will protect what God has given me to the fullest. If you touch me, I will touch you plain and simple, so please don't make me act in a way that may cause grief. So, let's get started as I am seeing things believing but not believing what I'm seeing being done before my very eyes. because it's surreal, but I know it's real, and he is watching and returning. I have been blessed by our Father in heaven with the holy spirit and wish to be even closer, and I'm going to continue to do what I must and enjoy this blessing, this feeling of being connected and nurture what he has given me and continue to praise him in his infinite mercy and love from above. Trying to avoid this madness in hopes that we live in his glory to glorify him.

What does it take for you to understand that racism or hatred in any form is born of your ignorance and lack of knowledge? You, who would believe that you are better than another, what reason do you commit this treason against each other when the actual fact is that in any color, race or breed you have those that exceed and those that don't, those that deceive and are deceitful and those that are true and truthful, not because of color not because of breed but because of who they are as a whole to have integrity or not is not defined by color. never a competition but coalition proof that we all are one for those that are free and able to see the truth that this division being divided has us lost and confused when united so much more we could be we who are your brothers and sisters no matter the color. What action can you do that cannot be done by another with the same knowledge or training? This sickness that you suffer this disease wanting to smother another because of color to gain power to see one cower, what joy is there in destroying another's dream hearing their screams?

When your Dream can as easily be destroyed. I find it appalling and while understanding things are out of hand as use these words to let you know what goes around comes around and you will pay for the crimes that you commit and the things you do to one another in this life. This is not all there is to be, this is just part of the journey as this misery is insane and the pain you cause to each other seems endless, whether for self-satisfaction or monetary gain, is ludicrous and you will pay accordingly if not in this life surely in the next.

As you read this text, know that there is more to come. Because of your own lack of morals or values, you commit such heinous actions to one another, causing grief and strife amongst families, friends, and nations for power or to gain political status. The stain you place on your soul the price you will pay in the end. Believe it or not, you will be judged by our creator in the end and pay for your actions you truly know this is not the end no matter your false bravado in acting like you don't believe or there is no final judgement. The suffering I see is uncalled for and undue to those that you force your will upon, and when that day comes, you cannot run and there is nowhere to hide because he sees and knows all don't cry why. He is in everything and everywhere, so take care from this day on in what you do to one another as we struggle and juggle our way through this life and journey to our destination. Stop wasting time on emotions of hate and anger causing pain and sorrow that leads down the road to inevitable destruction. Pay heed to the deeds that are done one and all.

Real Women

Are there any real women left that don't play emotional games of chess and test the boundaries of love between man and woman and truly know what they want and not guessing on how to keep a real man when they find one? When the choice of companion no longer is out of love and compatibility, but out of monetary need and gain, the pain (is too great) that is caused when blindly choosing one's mate for materialistic reasons instead of true value and morals.

Wondering why you cry when you chase after the one that beats you and treats you like trash when it was only about cash and status, but you walk over the one who cares and values you for who you really are not just your physical attributes. You ignore every facet of their being if the money is endless. Can this be what has become of society and its values with the marketing of sexuality? We wonder why so much lust and rape are being committed by all ages. The diseases and the jealousy as emotions run rampart. When games of the heart are being played with no remorse or worry about the consequences and sex is used as a weapon for monetary gain and becomes meaningless, the long-term effects of the degradation of what should be precious between two lovers becomes the norm between any who are together lessening the value of intimacy between true love and lovers.

Man or Woman

I, for one, do not condone this so-called gay revolution but I am not judge nor jury to each his own as I do not force my views upon you do not try and force me to believe something is right when its wrong. We are grown, and you sow the seeds of your own demise and no surprise to me in what I see, and you should be happy with how God has made you—woman and man! Not to be man on man or woman on woman. Just know I am not judging, but let's see if I can explain how I feel. I mean, you have a woman wanting to be a man but not liking men now. If that is not wrong or imbalance, then what is? You have a man wanting to be a woman but not liking women?

Seriously? Imbalanced, not happy with how God made you seriously, but you have pride in being gay and happy with what you say you are but not in how you were made? SMDH (shaking my damn head).

But again, I am not here to judge, just my thoughts and to each his own. I do not condone nor condemn but don't expect me to say it is okay when it is not plain and simple. What can be done when society itself supports or condones such reckless uncaring actions that split people into fraction and factions of what we should be? As I begin to see the domino effect it is having on nations and foundations, the catastrophe that is coming will not be avoided if not rectified. Be forewarned, we are on our way down the wrong road and show no signs of remorse for this course or the transgressions that are being committed. As the line becomes blurred with sexual orientation becoming a thing of choice not birth. When uncomfortable in one's own skin choosing to be something else other than what you were born as. Claiming pride in who you are yet not happy with how you were born to be man or woman.

Interracial Dating

Why does it matter if you date someone of a different race or color? Claiming race purity or not wanting to dilute one's gene pool foolish thoughts. As some of the most beautiful are of mixed heritage while others are deformed due to inbreeding and the like. If it was not meant to be, then it would not be like two men cannot have a child without adoption or two women cannot have a child without adoption or artificial insemination. This life is too short for such nonsense. Why should it matter? What should matter is that if there is love and compassion between two of opposite sex and color, race should not be an issue or factor. For those that choose to date outside of their own race, what business or concern is it of yours? Are you that unhappy and insecure with yourself that you involve yourself in another's private affairs? Maybe you need to do a little soul and self-searching and find out what makes you so undesirable? So, into another's affairs not managing your own issues when it really is none of your concern, or care being judgmental others personal lives is none of your concern. Is it because you see two people sharing a bond you do not have or that you want? Maybe if you weren't so self-centered or picky and dated outside your own, you could find that one true love that has been eluding you. If you weren't so blind and narrow-minded, your chances of true love and happiness would be open to more opportunities, but by closing your mind to this, you slim your own chances. Refusing to see that love is blind and knows no color limitations or materialistic boundaries, true love between man and woman is special and not to be constricted by color or race.

Misplaced Love

How can you claim to love me when you choose actions that continuously cause me pain? Saying that I am the only one for you has proven to be untrue. As the truth is revealed and Hidden secrets that produce darker lies that easily break the ties of love we once shared. One fleeting moment or two of weakness that lead to a minute of lust that destroyed our bond of trust now when I see you; I am filled with disgust for how I misplaced my trust, thinking that you cared, but finally realizing that you were never truly there. Like a fading dream that slips away at the waking of dawn, a memory or moment eventually to be forgotten, is how I wish that part of my life could so easily be erased. But then, when I am faced with the same situation, I would be unaware and blind, so I find that to Forgive but not Forget and to have learned about the games that can so easily be played and the lies that are easily told on the tip of the tongue may have at one time caused me pain.

But to have gained a better perspective and stronger grip upon my own feelings and emotions no longer drowning in an ocean of uncontrollable grief or sorrow for a love I thought was forever yet was never meant to be, I can now be free and hold a firm grip on the reigns of my life, no longer living with strife or raging emotions once again in control of myself. I am traveling upon the right path, being able to laugh once again through the sorrow through the pain, knowing there is a better and brighter day in my future as my goals and dreams come to light.

God has blessed me in his infinite might and wisdom, and for that, I am forever grateful to our Creator and my Savior as I look for my queen. So, as I begin carving a piece of this pie, the so-called American dream which seems to be an illusion a mirage scene off in the distance, I will have my fill as I take hold and mold these words like clay and pray, I find the one I can hold dear and near to my heart. As I part these waves and crave to be free of the misery, I see surrounding everyone due to greed, lust, envy, and jealousy for what another has. I thank the Lord in heaven for guiding me and providing me with whatever I have and need and have heeded my own greed, trying to pay heed to his laws and asking for forgiveness when I fall ever so short.

At my victory I begin to switch gears with no fears year after year, watching beers poured out for lost peers as I clear my mind and find my voice to speak out while seeking out the one for me and the truth amongst so many lies. Who could she be? as I am tired of the trickery and games because I am looking for my queen in these last days of lost values and morals? I care for a true union, me and you, under God, not a fraud. But chosen by God to be a caretaker, not a faker but a nurture of creation, not a destroyer like so many others and nations.

As I take it slow and grow this feeling, so intoxicating while invigorating, there is no debating there are no challengers or taking as it is a gift from above not to be bought, fought or sold. I thank him and praise him always, our Creator, Father and Savior! So, there is no competition, letting lose my pain to gain a grip through it all to stand tall giving praise to our Savior and Creator always and forever.

Taking flight with no fright to heights, none could have ever dreamed or imagined. I have seen and experienced things that have amazed me to his presence and grace and so have others on my journey with me. Slowly realizing the trials and tribulation I have gone through to mold me into the man I am today and no remorse for the pain, for I have gained so much from each and every situation to have learned my lesson and gained such a blessing in return.

Control

*T*his I write for you whether many or few as I at first tried to care, but now that I see ever so clearly this year. I will no longer allow myself to be bound by the mental chains of humanity, and its insanity is enough to drive anyone to the edge as I dredge up these charges. And society wonders why when the morals and principles of life are no longer taught to the youth. Some of these being compassion and love for their fellow beings, my only role model or story worth believing is that of my Savior being the reason I have minded my behavior thus far. You wonder why we have fallen so far from grace when each and every place has taken his teachings away. I pray for a better day, but what way is there when you cater to atheist and other religions that don't show such values and morals.

I again say to you, what can you find wrong with the Ten Commandments or Jesus Christ and his teaching? What can you find wrong in any of this? So why not teach it and let it be heard? You, who don't believe, you deceive yourself and others with your lustful ways and wayward actions, but you will not deceive me. So, the values and morals of life taught to youths in school nowadays as his teachings are no longer taught, whether in schools or at home and you wonder why our children act the way they do when there is no foundation given. But what is being built on sand and things are out of hand now that we take stock in Glock's and gangs, but not taking stock in our Savior and Creator, which is greater than all other things that matter? And you chatter about why we die and why we go through what we go thru? How can you even form your mouth around such words as why?

What help are the politicians that are for sale to the highest bidder in their campaigns to gain power? They gain wealth and power while selling you lies so easily told off the tip of their tongues. Your pleas for help and change fall upon deaf ears. Their six-figure paycheck paid by your taxes ye minimum wage to be raised is a battle. We pay them to keep us bound while they run around and decide our fate. I say, no more, I have grown and decide my own path to follow. I refuse to swallow their hollow words of caring and equality when the quality of life they have made for us causes strife and racial tensions that are brewing to the point of boiling over at an alarming rate. Will we continue to allow these immoral deeds to degrade us as humans when we have more sense than this? To live currently in this day and age that has reverted to common savagery and barbarians, what use is intelligence and common sense if you do not learn and change from wicked ways of the past and misdeeds done long ago?

Who Is to Blame?

How is it when something bad happens, we blame the devil or ask God why he let this happen? Do we not understand the gift that was given to choose which road you take? If everything was predestined, then what good would the gift of free will be or the chance to be forgiven for living the way we do. As for asking God why he let this happen, God did not make us to control our actions. We do what we do to ourselves being faithless, nonbelievers, and simply not caring. We have been given many teachings living and written examples of how we should act or treat each other, but it seems we refuse to listen or pay attention to the signs given.

And as for the power the devil holds, the only power he holds over you is the lies and half-truths told to you that you listen to, which you either choose to ignore or believe in and that which you let him have by letting him mislead you into actions to go against what teachings and examples our Creator has shown us to live by. It is your choice, your decision, a gift given. Not to be forced or controlled but to have the chance and opportunity to choose for ourselves what road we take and mistakes we make and to be forgiven if we choose to ask for forgiveness and wish to change. So again, it is we who allow this to happen to us. It is we, who choose to be thus, but in the end, it is our Creator who will judge us on our actions and choices made, not you or me with our bias opinions of each other. It is we, as humans, who do this to each other with our lack of respect for life and concern of each other's well- being. And as for myself, I believe this is just the first part of life in which we live where my actions, now and here, determine what happens to my soul that my Creator breathed into me and blessed me with to be a part of him and his creation, which I am very grateful and thankful for.

Preordained

How can you explain life as preordained and then claim we were given free will that would mean it is fruitless to try or ask for forgiveness that we live this way? As I pray for understanding, I have come to realize a few things. While the confusion you try to cause allows me to see the flaws in the things or laws you propose and implant to divide and conquer and keep those who would oppose you off balance and confused, I refuse to continue falling for such tactics or antics, no matter your supposed consequences because the offenses you commit are worse than the degradation and dehumanization in the name of a higher cause. The flaws that are ever present and clear, the imminent danger as I break free of the chains you have tried to place on me and my mentality in this reality. I see the fatalities daily and no longer caught in stasis with what you try. I am tired of the lies and the games as I bring to bear this gift and lift my head and write these words and say you tread down the road to your own demise with no surprise. You continue to ply the only trade you know and receive a failing grade. You are being weighed and measured and are found to be wanting with your taunting and abuse of power. I see it unraveling before our very eyes, and as I begin traveling this earth, I tell you to reverse your course or there is hell to pay for the games you play. The day is coming soon, whether you believe it or not in this land you have taken for your own and have sown seeds of discord amongst many. How canny is this game you are playing, feeding your own greed by living off the back of others sweat, pain, and misery? As I gain entry and grab hold and mold these words to bring to bear, that which I see is wrong currently and wage this war, I thank my Lord for this gift he has given me. I begin to unsheathe my blade, and it is shining Bright. heads will roll and foundations will crumble as I rumble in this jungle. There will be more to come, as I am not done yet. And if one hair is to be harmed on this, I will be sure to tell our Creator unlike my Savior. You know what you do and have done, When the time comes for judgement. As I see through you like glass, transparent to the bone you have shown the truth in your actions not the hollow words you serve out of your mouth.

Do You Know Love?

Do you really know how to love? You claim to know what you want from a relationship, but when you receive what you ask, you take for granted the one that would be kind and treat you how you deserve to be treated. You wonder why you can never find a mate for your soul. You don't even know your true desires. I am tired of hearing such cries of woe when you know within yourself the true reason born out of materialistic wants and lust. The trust that is easily broken by misdeeds done whether for greed or lust are you joking with yourself or with me as this is not how it should be. Outer beauty instead of inner values, and morals of a person that would lead to a lasting meaningful relationship worth having and keeping. It seems that the love is lost when we get comfortable and forget to do the little things we used to do when we first met and falling head over heels for each other. If you truly understood love, then it would never die, lie, or cheat. Unimportant matters would take a seat to what truly is important—the well-being and support of each other in hard times and good. It would be understood that supporting you is supporting me and vice versa. Whatever it took in the beginning to keep your partner satisfied and in love would never stop, change, or leave. You would not deceive or leave for another if truly in love. Instead of taking the easy way out and giving up, not living up to the qualities of being a man or woman and taking care of home. Currently, as the sexual intensity to satisfy one's hunger for more is made harder, unfortunately, the fact seems to be those that do try are taken for granted and efforts are unappreciated.

So, how do you treat one who would meet you at the door with fresh roses and have your bath water prepared when you came home from a hard day's work and massage your feet after working all week? One who would never tire of expressing his desire to please you in every way? Everyday doing the best that he can to show how much he appreciates and cares for the trust and love you have placed in him, even though he may not have the monetary means to fully support you, but brings enough to the table that suffices surviving and maintaining a household together. Treating you like a queen, but you do not treat him like a king, but continuously bring him grief. Caring for your emotional and personal needs, but greed as you're thinking that the grass is greener on the other side when it really is not. As you complete me and I complete you, what do we do? Does it matter to you at all to stand tall at my side or leave by the wayside?

Happiness and Joy

What does happiness and joy mean to you? Is it when you have money? When you have the power to control others' lives? Or is it something that cannot be bought or sold, something you hold inside that can only be gained from a deeper understanding of oneself that no one else can destroy your joy? There is satisfaction in knowing that you are growing and doing your best. Believe that someone will test your balance and try to destroy your joy, but if you take solace in a strong foundation built on a rock and not sand, then you can understand that no man or woman can take your joy away no matter the situation or what you are facing while chasing your dreams. It is amazing how misery loves company and causing the pain of others in order to feel better about themselves for a fleeting moment that they must continue. Such actions can never be truly rewarding, avoiding the inevitable fact that they do not know how to act or find happiness in their own life, seeking to cause strife and fill the emptiness inside themselves with actions of hate, only to deepen their fate. Time always tells the toll. You reap what you sow by your own actions and intentions. What you do returns tenfold in ways you can't even imagine at the time, as what goes around comes around. So why do you surround yourself with such actions of degradation and separation? Violations committed against another for personal gain to bring them pain, you find pleasure in this. It is never truly satisfying or gratifying hence the continuous need to commit such deeds.

It blackens the soul and keeps you on a road of emptiness. A void of blackness that you can't escape only gets deeper and darker to the point where you are totally lost beyond redemption. Wake up (if you do not make a U-turn) and see the light or error of your ways.

Try

I used to try and reach you because I felt a connection, thinking it was natural selection. But after recollection, it was the wrong choice. It was never meant to be. It definitely was not worth the misery. I endured trying to show you how much I cared, taking for granted the things I tried to share with you. Never will you find one that would have given his all to see you live your dreams. Instead, you schemed on ways to play games to shame me or blame me. Playing games of the heart to tear my world apart, using games of the mind and being unkind, finding that everything you said or claimed was a lie to help you get by. You wonder why life is so hard and that everyone you meet does not treat you with respect. Well, it's for the hell you caused and the way you act. You refuse to understand that not only must you love yourself if no one else, but you must also have respect for yourself. Your lack of respect in the way you act in public places, with no concern for your disrespectful mannerism that impress only those that have the same dysfunction as you, show the ignorance you possess. What do you think you want to prove when you *take for granted the one who treats you with the love you want and deserve, but yet, you show such disgust or distaste to disgrace someone willing to spend his or her last to pull you through the muck and you chuck it all away for one or more days of carnal pleasure in these trying times and crimes of passion fashion long-lasting feelings of remorse or regret when you look back on how you acted in haste and wasted what could have been everlasting?*

Why is Life So Complicated?

The complications in life at times can be very depressing and unnerving. It would seem to me from my own perspective and insight that not only is it due to the internal conflict and complexity, but also the external as well. If you take the time to do some internal evaluations of oneself and truly list the pros and cons with an unbiased view of what you do, if at all possible, taking note of one's own iniquities to truly understand the internal aspects and complications in one's life that brings strife and some to the point of breaking while making irreparable mistakes that take a toll and cause undue damage. What does it take as you look long and hard at yourself and companions? Do they harm or hinder one's progression to becoming a better individual or compliment one's attributes with endearing qualities of their own? Your companions can cause your life to have many complications that could easily be avoided if you pay attention to the actions and intentions, they show you not with what they say but what they do, which would be part of the external factor, if the lives they live and portray are in contrast with your own due to jealousy and envy of what you have and what they do not have but can achieve if they try. There is some truth in what is said. You are like those you choose to be around unless you are of stronger will and nature; a leader, not a follower. Like crabs in a barrel, eventually, you get pulled back down into the muck unless being helped up, instead of dragged down and clowned. I see through my eyes that even though life is complicated and hard, there are things one can do for one's self that can alleviate and address most situations to ease the stress that is being felt. As I have knelt and prayed for a better way and better day, one should try to better evaluate what is being done not only in themselves, but also around them and stop playing, using and abusing another to gain moments of fame or monetary gain that brings another pain to the brink of losing it all. To make one fall to get ahead is not the way to be and will only bring misery and pain for a moment's gain because, in the end, what goes around, comes around worse than before.

Do You Really Think It's a Game?

*H*ave *you not realized yet that it's far from being a game when playing with someone's mind? Do they have to find you face down in the ground in a pool of blood for playing? someone like a fool? No longer will I tolerate anyone who would think to violate my mentality or reality with such games. It is a shame to you and me to play in such a manner. So, I lock away that side, which resides in me, to have such hate. Make no mistake as I am a Gemini no excuse as I categorize the abuse and take note you try my patience with such antics and games. And I am growing tired of the continuous lies Committed with malice, not Alice in wonderland. And we blunder the wonder of creation our station to be nurturers and caretakers, not such destroyers. So, as I choose to live and forgive but not forget, don't make me act a fool. You know the rules as before.*

And now as I ply my trade, you shall be weighed and measured as I treasure this life and blessing, he has given us to be living here and enjoy as it is a paradise lost but can be regained if we change our ways, before it is too late, and we pay the price for acting trifle with life. But trust and believe there is no twice go - round as I break down these walls and facades this game of charades as you parade around. You don't want a showdown or hoedown. You don't want to throw down seriously. It's not a game. And you play it as a joke as people get smoked way too often laid in a coffin, showing no pity for the shitty way we treat each other with no respect. And you expect shit to change, and you stay the same, showing no shame with the games you play, manipulation in every nation, attacking the foundations getting caught red-handed, thinking you can escape like a bandit when the planet gets caught up in the aftermath of the war you cause with dirty tactics and laws that are severely flawed and the day is coming to light, where right and wrong are misconstrued with news told wrong or guessing games being played.

This is not a façade or charades. We are headed in the wrong direction, so as I begin my dissection like a surgeon and purging the lies, I see with truth as I know it, will you continue to blow it and throw it all away with the way you play as I am done with these games and lies? I am blessed yet stressed, and I am blessed by our Creator and our Savior with the spirit and hold it near and dear and I do not fear any of you, as I will do to you as you do to me if you continue, and you will pay the price, not me. You will burn if you do not learn because it's not a game the framework is being laid you have played once to often, it's not a joke. Life is a gift and a blessing, and I find deceit at every turn. Will you learn or burn what is the true agenda, trying to hold on to power as the hour draws near and the corruption is evident and ever so present in politics and government? The finger pointing, name-calling, and game playing are sickening.

How long do you think people will fall sway as I pray it gets better and not worse with this mass confusion? I begin this transfusion to hopefully avert what I see coming down the road, if things are not changed and made right. I light this beacon of hope as this nation supposedly under God let such fraudulent things continue. Catering to godlessness and atheism in schools and every corner, rocking the foundation of this nation that should and could be so much more, allowing unions of man on man and woman on woman like the horrors of Sodom and Gomorra. Do we not learn from past mistakes? It is not a game or a joke, so be warned. I see the lust and disgust of it all, but I am not one to judge. But I am giving you forewarning as you disregard the laws of our God in heaven. And wonder why things go awry in this live. I see the signs of times ever so clearer as it draws nearer to an end and new beginning.

What Are You Looking for?

*I*t seems like everyone is searching for something and looking at me one way or another. So, as I say, I am here and yes, I am blessed by our Creator with the spirit and I am thankful to have received such a gift from our Father in heaven and our Savior, so I try to mind my behavior. I am by far not perfect. I have my faults yet do my best to treat others with respect until given a reason not to, I do give praise to our savior and creator and raise him above this mess that I see that surrounds me and tries to grind me down. I won't be deceived! The gift that he has given me It can't be stolen or taken, no faking in me. I'm not giving up or giving in nor throwing it away. As I raise my head up and say do not play these games as it shames you, him, and me but most of all you. I have maintained my cool because I am not a fool and don't make me act like one, because I have no fear of you, and I will protect that which he has given me by any means necessary.

I do not wish to have you buried in a casket with your head blown like a gasket drastic measure for the things that you do. I have not done a thing to harm you, but you twist and pull, pick and pry, so as I ply my trade, I warn you of these things. I see and hear innuendoes while seeming oblivious I'm taking note and through these eyes recording the games and lies being played, and as I begin to nip things in the bud for the rude treatment and disregard, respect is given, not earned but if you give me a reason to not respect you for the treatment received then so be it as this hell grows hot from the antics and games you continue to play. I grow tired of biting my tongue and holding back these words that need to be said. As I begin to let it out in one way or another rather than smothering my brother or sister as I mold these words like clay and form a way to release my own anger, frustration and tension laying down a foundation built on rock taking stock in my savior. I'm free to say what is needed and pray each day in one way or another, asking my Father in heaven to forgive me for my own indiscretions. I say to you as you seem to know what you do, watch your mouth your snickering, whispering, and judging. You do not want me to be judge and jury as my fury is forthwith and coming? If you continue in such a manner my anger knows no bounds. I could begin from the bottom to the top beginning to end. So many angles in this tangled web you weave to deceive. The gift I have received is a blessing, not a curse as things seem to be going in reverse.

So many cultures; so many breeds, and it is one deed that planted one seed, that opened gate which allows this hate and greed to take root in your soul as I watch it grow from the smallest place. I can read you at a glance watching your stance from a distance. You are transparent like glass in your expressions and words. You think I do not hear far from deaf. I could be blunt and say you can kiss it. Who the hell are you to judge? You really think you are better or have the right? So, should I feel the same way? Looking at me, as if you have the authority, did you try to be civil like I have? Have you said hi, how are you doing? Can I help you? What is wrong? Like I have many a times just out of actual simple concern for your state of being. The few that know me and talk to me know my mannerism and how kind and helpful I try to be just for the fact it's the right way to conduct oneself. You stare and smirk, whisper and judge, saying slick things out the side of your neck forcing me to check my own anger, thinking you are cute when you are not. Quite a few of you think it's funny or a game, in truth, you should be ashamed. The nerves to claim things untrue. the audacity you know who you are.

We wonder why our world is being torn asunder as we blunder through life like a bull in a China shop, or why so many lose their minds with the unkind actions and words easily done to each other currently. If you walked a mile in my shoes, you probably would have been dead by now by your own hand if not others. While I'm protected and blessed by The Most High my Adonai, so I try to maintain a certain level of decorum. Do you honestly believe the true Creator of the entire splendor and wonder of what you see every day when you open your eyes and truly look would condone such or support any of these snickers, whispers and actions of disgust from any faction that aimlessly destroys life that is precious? Let me stop here and say, whether you believe or not does not make it so, I continue to pray for you to see the error in your ways. Open your eyes as the days are numbered and the hour is coming. For the hate and ignorance, I see astounds me, as our world stands on the edge of this ravine for the crimes committed around the globe as more and more turn away from the truth and light of our Creator, who is greater than you or me in the entire universe, alpha and omega. You ask why all the woes as the lack of belief and faith grows at an astounding rate the lack of values, morals and respect rises, and you believe this is it this all there is to be in this existence.

I wish you the best as you test and jest lying to yourselves in these last days as I watch the wicked ways of mankind continue. The big bang, theory of evolution is distortion of the truth as it takes a balance of all to make it work not chance or luck as some would have us believe look at the design of it all for life to thrive and survive a balance is needed. The Precision and placement of everything is proof enough for me of our Creator as what is needed for life to exist and maintain its existence, so believe what you will. I will not be deceived by any. As I give praise to our Creator and my Savior for who I am, what I am, and what I will be.

Creation

To be bound by man-made restrictions and constrictions, binding yourself to that which you can feel, touch, or see and there is much more to you and me than the eye can see more than you and I could ever imagine. If I was to go by others train of thought, then these words I write are nothing but meaningless prattle. But as I do not allow myself to be blinded or bound by these thoughts or words and I have seen and felt so much more than you can imagine or hope. I have been blessed with the gift to express myself in such a way that I will simply say in no way do I presume to think that I am above or better than you in any way, but I will plainly say that goes in reverse or vice versa as well. You have had your fun and played your games, but the time is done the game is over though I may still have residual echoes. I am awake, and no fake no snake as I make it known loud and clear not only with these words but proof in my actions past, present and future. you are not slick, I won't be tricked in this life as I strive to survive this mess watching the games and lies being played endlessly, *seeking my true wife and queen. You can screw around if you want. I won't taunt or flaunt the fact that I am blessed no matter the stress and what I go through. Don't want your cash, jewels, or materialistic things. I do find myself intrigued as it seems I have been given such a gift that my perception of things would seem drastically out of place while I watch humankind race toward destruction at such a pace no trace of slowing. I truly feel sorrow for those that chose to lose as they refuse to believe only to deceive themselves. as I gratefully receive my gift that has been given to be forgiven while living a promise to all that choose to believe. That is really all it takes to not be a snake or fake. Wake up and accept that which our Creator offers, accept him and his forgiveness that our Savior died to provide us with a connection a bond that had been broken so long ago. And we continue to neglect and abuse the fact that we have such an opportunity for unity and not be divided as we are. So many ask and wonder how things could happen as they do. if you truly believe and accept him, does he care? Yes, he does, As I truly know and accept this and prove this in my own mannerism and actions even though wild and at times very mild, we all have our doubts and questions seeking answers to questions in life as we struggle to understand and comprehend. But I know and truly believe and accept my Father in heaven and as my Lord, God, Elohim and his son as Savior. The only reason I have minded my behavior and been gifted as such. Who is it who has turned their back? It has been us, not him. He has proven his love for us time and again, and we have fallen short and far from his grace time and time again. But he is ever loving, merciful and kind. If you choose to find your way back to him and stop these* actions of godlessness and lack of faith and take your place in creation, your station to be caretakers and nurturers, not destroyers full of lust and greed, and pay heed to his laws and his teachings as he is reaching out to us yet time and time again so what should we do? We have been given lesson after lesson, rule after rule, and guide after guide? But we don't seem to care, listen or pay attention, so I bid you farewell as you would do well to worry as we bury body after body, friend after friend, father after father, son after son, mother after mother, and daughter after daughter. Ready or not, sooner or later, I can't even imagine what fate awaits as I debate my own course of actions. I feel I could pay you back with ease for how you tease me and abuse me mentally with threats of fire and stone as I am grown you shall reap what you have sown. And I thank my Father in heaven for that which I can call my own, which he has given me to cherish, I will not let it perish. As I begin to open up and let you know, I see how you act, the things you say behind my back, and the games you play. It is not a game I am playing. You are laying your own seed of discord and you reap what you sow, so continue if you wish this game. How will it end? Where will it lead as I pray for you? But I tell you, I know what you do, and when I go, I will say, 'Father, they know what they do. They know what they have done, and it is time they pay for the way they disregard life and its precious gift!"

Weapons

Using man-made weapons against each other, thinking it proves you're a man. You would have me believe this makes you a man/thug/bad boy because you need a man-made weapon that easily destroys life to prove your worth when indeed it shows your lack thereof, as we know it. As I said before, I give thanks to my Lord that I have been given a different perception and won't fall for the misconception. I will use it for protection but nothing else. If I must watch your head bust with disgust, I will do so in dismay as I pray that day never comes, and know I see no pleasure in seeing one die laying by the wayside for transgression committed or a simple act of greed. It seems to be used in schemes for accumulating cream causing screams of terror shattering dreams of kings and queens into pieces as life ceases.

There is no way to put it nicely. The only way you can get your issue across it seems is to be a pistol-packing fool, using a tool of destruction to make people see your way of things. But as I bring to bear this gift of a different perception, how does using a weapon make you a man? what have you to say about your actions as you so easily extinguish life with actions so, sickening? using a pistol or knife taking a Life which is precious and should be cherished. The truth and cold fact, while running with your pack of wolves or armies and acting hard, I'm pulling your card. You are not gods, but boys with toys of pain, proving nothing but showing how childish your actions are, factions, and fractions of what we could be in this day and age as war wages across the globe and the manner in which you choose to display your aggressions.

While he is watching, you show no shame in your choice of actions. So, as I lift my head and write words that need to be seen and said as to what I see before me, you condemn yourselves with your actions. You act so hard with your pack of hyenas nothing but savage scavenger's, hurting innocent men, women and children. With weapon in hand making, you feel like a man, when you are weak and childish? Even a small child can hold and fire a gun. So, proven with the news of children doing such things currently. I would think myself being a man constitutes using one's brain not only for gain but knowing how to refrain from such callous and heartless actions that cause others undue pain just for gain, being able to maintain and sustain a lifestyle without having to use or abuse another in the process. But who am I? I am but a blip on the radar in this life we live watching the days go by as I try to explain what I see going awry. I could just cry not only tears of sorrow, but tears of frustration as I watch the annihilation of life, whether it is because of greed or lust, white or black, red or yellow. To lose a fellow human being to such crimes is disgusting, whether child, man, or woman. It is hard for me to understand how this leads to the claim of being a gangster man or thug or being hard. It is weak, demeaning, and childish such actions for one's own satisfaction. Proving not that you are Men, Gangster or hard core but Cowardly resorting to such tactics to get one's way or issue across to another. Instead of using words choosing vicious actions and tactics that are childish in nature. Being a man Being grown is Being able to accept being Wrong apologizing and trying to rectify or pacify any given situation. Also, when right knowing what to say how to say it without antagonizing, instigating or making another feel belittled.

Confusion

Can you even attempt to understand how you had me confused as one minute is okay to express how I feel, then the next it is not? My feelings will not be misled as I tread thru this life watching the strife caused from uncaring actions, slowly gaining a hold and understanding my place while landing these blows. I will not stop but continue as I have been given this gift while living this life to see thru your deception. What reception have I received from smiles to smirks while I walk this path that I tread Alone but never truly alone filled with the spirit guarded by our creator's angel's. Like an infrared beam my eyes glare at your very own stare, and you dare to presume or judge. Do not make look your way as I will lay you low with every blow laying bare all the things that you do. You are transparent like glass, down to the very core of your soul with every expression you make every action your take, revealing your inner emotions and true feelings on your face that cannot be hidden while dealing these blows in every direction. I aim to ease this pain as I grab hold *refusing to fold from one day to the next. I am vexed with the looks and the stares as if you dare to judge or compare faking like you care as I return your stare. Should I do the same as I could lay blame right at your door for your atrocious actions and games of misdirection trying to hold me down or push me the wrong way? But I do not play games with life issues. I pray that I do not have to act out of place, and leave your body traced in chalk for idle talk or whispered words of ignorance while I hold back these feelings of anger and frustration for violations committed with no regard for the pain that they cause. How I could just pay you back in kind for such actions. It is not a game I ignore the ignorance for your benefit as well as mine as I begin to shine the light on all that you do. Believe me, if you feel what I feel know what I know, then it is not a game and you shame yourself, me, and our Creator with the things that you do with malice intent. Because I will not be contained, held down, back, or led astray as I pray each day for a way through this mess that's before my very eyes. From what I see, what I feel, I know he is real and coming back, however he chooses and whenever he chooses his will not mine be done. I have chosen the winning side, so watch what you do! I tell you one last final time it is not a game life is not a joke. As people play each other like chess pushing pieces on the board of life with no care who is laid to rest.*

The Love for Me

*W*ill I ever find the one who is right for me, a love that is true no matter what we go through? It seems obvious to me in this time or place, I face unbeatable odds with so; many frauds playing games their whole character a facade. I feel lost in a world where love and compassion are unknown, Morales and Values lost a concept from ages long past it would seem. As I have grown throughout the years overcoming any fears and trying to love again, I wonder in the end if true love really exists. As I remain persistent in my constant search, for one like me in this day and age, where morals and values no longer exist in a relationship and respect for one another's feelings are of no concern and burned by the wayside where it's all about me no union, no compromise, or communication causing strife between man and wife with feelings of animosity toward each other where none should be. For me, what place is there in this world as I have tried time after time to be the one that is different, showing more than I should, trying to care but receiving in return nothing but lies and *deceit? While growing sick to the core and searching for a love that is pure. While the only cure I see for what ails me is to allow my feelings and emotions to fade and grow cold and uncaring, daring you to cross me as I show you in return the things that I find that you have shown me becoming harsh and callous my only concern is of me is that how I must be in this day and age? Do as you wish to be done and be paid back in kind is what I'm finding to be the only remedy for this malady. Slowly to let go of trying to show any different then the way you treat me even though two wrongs don't make it right but letting you continue to get away with actions that cause pain with no change in your own does no justice to me or you. So, as I regain control of my own actions and emotions and begin to put an end to any games being played mentally or physically. Getting a grip and removing anything that is not constructive or uplifting from my presence or circle.*

Blessed

I am blessed by the Most High My Adonai and give praise always to my Creator, Lord and Savior. Though my behavior may be sporadic and wild at times as I climb from the bottom, have you forgotten while plotting my demise as I rise from the ashes like a phoenix to be reborn yet torn in twain from the pain and joy I feel being gifted yet dumbfounded while feeling hounded, grounded, and pummeled mentally and physically but not yielding, nor bending yet maintaining and gaining more than I ever imagined, as I begin to use these words given to me to escape the misery, I see surrounding me. I thank the Lord above who is my only judge for his love, mercy, and compassion and these words that I use to display the gift given to me. As he resides within me and all around and provides me with everything I need, sustaining me through these dark times when most needed as I watch the spark within me grow to a point, I cannot contain the shine nor should I while praying as I grow older, and mold these words, I feel that need to be heard. I serve our Father in

heaven and thank him for everything that I have been through and experienced good and bad, for my blessings and lessons I have learned while yearning to be more. that these games you play with lives that you have taken for granted from the seed planted long ago to whom do you show your allegiance with this continuous lust and greed, you deceive yourselves but not me. I have tried time and again, as I'm far from being perfect, but and still have shown love compassion and mercy at times that I really shouldn't have and where none has been shown to me. I have turned my cheek each week not meek nor weak as I begin to speak out. I have no doubt that what I have felt is real. No façade and no game of charades are being played as my cards are laid on the table not a fable nor fiction with so many contradictions. Being True to myself My Elohim, My Savior and His Blessings while living life learning lessons from past mistakes to move forward and be free.

Proud American

So proud American, see if you can explain to me how it could be that, for one you atone for the atrocity committed by the Nazis to the Jews in the holocaust and the capture of their gold and art. By out-of-court settlement, you atone for the bombing of Hiroshima that killed many in the first world war, even though they bombed Pearl Harbor; you even atone to the Native American for decimation of tribes and vicious purging of the Native American and the stealing of their land. But how have you atoned to Black America and Africans (you now call African Americans) which you took from Africa to make your slaves to build this country. The Destruction of the Black Wall Street in Tulsa where so many innocent lives were taken, and property destroyed and stolen...They were enslaved, persecuted viciously, killed, abused, raped, and murdered, and still, to this day, suffer the indignation and slights from white America and had to struggle and fight for over four hundred years, Through discrimination and segregation and more to build this nation, fifty to sixty years of half-ass education and so-called help is supposed to *make up for four hundred years of miseducation, oppression and abuse. Do not make me laugh at such a farce. Yet we still make it through because we are blessed even though abused and mistreated greeted with dirty looks by the true crooks who have stolen history trying to rewrite the past. While you and your descendants enjoy the fruits of their blood-soaked labor and most of us suffer to survive and you would call us uncivilized and portray us as animals and criminals, but we are a product of abuse and lack of reparations in education.*

Affirmative action is all you have to offer. Still some groan about that being in use and how long has that even been in effect. How is that supposed to correct the lack of respect and the degradation of a nation you caused with your dirty and duplicitous laws and the pain and the fear you inflicted, and the feeling of inferiority you beat into a whole nation? And still, we strive to make it through the backstabbing of our own as well as so many others because of the visual lies and propaganda. I see reparations made to all, but we and our homeland that you have raped and pillaged as if you feel not only entitled but as if we are of no consequence or that you have the right because of the color of your skin your lack of pigmentation. How wrong you are so far from the truth it's saddening and sickening. You still feel no need to rectify the situations and tensions you have caused. I, for one, see something wrong with this picture. Not asking for a handout don't need or want nothing but the respect that is due that you will give or in return be shown the same disrespect you show.

So, this that you have done, is enough to take away the feeling of being lost and hopeless in a country that shows lack of concern or respect for the descendants of those who helped build and shape this so-called great nation that you have today?

Such logic to me seems a slap in the face to me and my race, but no matter your tricks or games that you continue to play, I pray for you and yours and mine to wake up. God willing, with or without help, I will make my way through this mess.

That I see, I have made my own mistakes, taken my spills and falls, but as I stand tall and have been through it all to speak out about what I see going on. God has blessed me, and I am thankful to our Creator and my Savior who I attribute to no color and not the pale blonde hair blue eyed images being displayed there is no way growing up in and around Egypt under the Sun, day in day out to lack color.

As I'm Carried through by his infinite mercy and grace to begin to take my place and shall continue with no fear. I do not see color. I see actions as we all are one, whether you see it or not. I see that we are brothers and sister no matter the color and our actions to each other must change for the better before it is too late as this hell is growing hot in this melting pot all over the globe!

You Would Claim to Be GOD?

So, you, who would claim to be God. You have much gall to claim that. Do you truly believe you are superior? In what ways? Intellect? Your claim of godship shows to me that you truly do not know your place or position in this cosmic composition. Even I being blessed, do not have the gall to claim other than that I am his creation, his child, and my station to be a nurturing and caretaker of creation and not a snake, destroyer, or fake. I have more to learn as I burn with a desire and fire that fuels my ire at those that would think they are high or higher than the one who has created us all in his image. I will not fall like the devil and his ilk by thinking I know better or am more for they lost long ago when cast out from heaven. And if you follow such a route no doubt the same will befall you, I feel sorry for you and hope you learn to change your ways and thoughts as you do not and cannot think that you are God and have the right to take life as you do. You will pay for such insolence as you may damage the flesh but not the soul and your soul will burn if you do not learn. As I am

embedded with sevens signed and sealed. Not only by my actions but by accepting my savior and creator and doing my best to follow his example as well as accepting him and his forgiveness of my own inadequacy and to be forgiven while trying to live this life free of strife that is rife with deception and misleading information.

But I digress as I will not fall that far from grace as to misplace my faith as I make a way through my clouded mind and times grow more troubled as disbelief and immoral ways grow more frequent even though you know and see the truth and the signs of the times. To those that chose to remain blind, trying to find your way through the dark, straying far from the light and the fold of his loving arms, as his spirit, we hold in each and every one of us, but him, we are not as our world grows hot and colder as the years fly by faster than we think. It seems most have forgotten or do not care as you dare to compare yourself to the one that gave his son so that even if you fall, you can get back up and stand tall. All that is needed is to accept him as your Lord and Savior and ask for forgiveness that we live this way do not pay attention to the images or paintings but the message that was sent for us to hear. As one of the basic commandments no engraven images or idols. And it seems with so many being displayed that cause so many to be turned away. Instead of focusing on the message that was brought to all of Humankind. All you must do is accept the salvation that is offered to you truly a gift. As the madness grows and the language barrier from Babel has been broken and communication once again flows freely between factions. Yet still we remain divided, fractions, undecided and lost in the wicked ways we choose to follow. Twisted by greed, jealousy, envy, and lust until turned to dust. While Hollow Callous Words

Lacking of faith and misplaced trust, refusing to believe, leads to being easily deceived being unable to receive relief, Or the Gift that is offered not only Material but spiritual in nature allowing the world in which we live fall further into disarray, the dismay I feel as I pray that you wake from this sleep and spell u seem to be under because we blunder the wonder of creation and our station to be caretakers and not destroyers. We wonder why we die or are allowed to suffer man, woman, or child blaming the devil or God. We were made free to choose what path we follow, whether straight and narrow or long and arduous. To believe and receive the gifts offered and given freely.

By simply showing love and compassion for each other while praising him who made us and honor and respect each other who are made in his image! But we show no trust and a lot of disgust, hate, and anger for our situation and pain that we suffer, asking why would he allow this to happen or for us to go thru what we do when it is our own actions, decisions, and lack of compassion that have caused any and all loss we have received, whether to ourselves and others what we choose what we do not only affects us but those around us in ways seen and unseen.

Why does God let this happen if he does exist? Because we are not robots to be controlled. We are not pets; we are his children and with your own children when you give them rules and they disobey you either punish them or let them learn the hard way what they are doing is wrong. the killing and abuse must stop. We have been taught and been given guidelines, but we refuse to use or follow them. We have examples and lessons of how we should act and treat each other, but we refuse to pay heed or attention, so how can we ask why or how this could happen?

We are killing ourselves with our own ignorance and lack of respect or discipline, saying we are grown and some thinking they are gods but acting like spoiled brats seduced by power, lust, and greed. Are you not punished for breaking the laws of the land you live in and for breaking the laws of our God, Creator, and Father, allowing the precious gift of life to be taken for granted, using and abusing each other? Instead of using all we have for a better brighter future for all we fall way short continuously making weapons of mass destruction to annihilate each other.

Scientifically stunted focused on destruction instead of advancement of all health and prosperity, perpetually committing actions that cause each other pain. The insanity of humanity claiming to be mankind, yet the kind seems to be missing. The fact some claim to be God's yet falling way short from the mark failing miserably at even being his children… Are you a Child of God or Child of the Deceiver…?

Your Flag and Nation's Foundation

I can no longer pledge allegiance to a flag and should not to a nation that lay false claims to be a nation under God, when its leaders are frauds and cheaters, allowing the foundation of this nation to fall, using and creating laws that undermine what was once a boon to its people. How can you claim to be unbiased or not catering to any religious faction, when in truth, your actions cater to atheist and nonbelievers first by banning prayer in schools, forcing those who wish to pray not to? Next, you allow laws that sanction same-sex marriage. It is bad enough that this union occurs, but to sanction its occurrence as legitimate and done by a nation under God? I have nothing against those that choose this union. To each his or her own, but I will not say I condone it or am fine with it. In my own opinion, it is not acceptable to say you have gay pride or such, when you have no pride in how you were made as man and woman. But I am not one to judge. It is just my own opinion and what I feel must be said as our father destroyed Sodom and Gomorrah for such atrocities, and *we wonder why things are happening now? As I won't force my view down your throat do not force yours down mine. And I hold no ill will or malice toward any gays or homosexuals. Believe me. It is just not my lifestyle or one that you will get me to say is okay or right when it is not. We are all human, and I presume not to judge, cause if you judge, so shall ye be judged. And to have on your money "In God We Trust" with your greed and lust for power that you use subversive tactics and propaganda to no end to keep people divided instead of united as that demonic face of racism you tried to hide is on the rise and you spend time, money, and effort to reform other nations and your own foundation continues to erode, making law after law with flaw after flaw, wasting people's hard-earned tax money for your own nefarious desires and agendas, faking concern for world peace with actions of deceit, what actual relief do you provide nations in turmoil, supplying rebels and insurgents whatever they need, if their agenda coincides with yours? And you have the nerve to sanction others that choose to do as you do?*

Does the term lead by example mean anything at all? I see an example you hide but is coming out in the open with all your scandals and mishandling of power in these last days! I pledge Allegiance to my Creator who is greater than us all. I do not hate but love this country will not disrespect the flag by burning or such nonsense, but u will not force me to pledge to a flag that supposedly represents freedom yet condones such egregious actions from its police, politicians and citizens. To uphold Duplicity, Deceit and continuous degradation of people of color as well as non-colored…. as the fact remains still America holds to a silent standard and indignation of entitlement to the elite lighter scheme of things. To say there is no Racism or White privilege is astoundingly naïve. Not only is it being shown by the 45th president but astonishingly it is either overlooked or endorsed by so many in this nation that you would have me pledge allegiance to a flag that does not respect or protect me and those of my color. Is not only laughable but an affront to my own intellect.

People of Color

You, at one time or another, call my people and I colored or people of color, etc., as we come in all shades from albino (Caucasian) white and too dark as night. As I glance from side to side, I must ask, while you can mask the lack of pigment with a tan, how can you say such things as I bring to bear these facts? I see when you get mad, you turn red. When you tan, you turn various shades of brown. When you bruise, you turn black and blue. So, I ask you, who is one of color? You are my kin even though your skin lacks my tone. We have grown so far apart that it breaks my heart at times. The callous crimes committed mainly by you but on both sides of the board. Whether you like it or not, we are all one race, one breed and one seed. We are just many shades that have been divided over the ages as war rages across the globe. Through these, I watch and learn. I must ask, are you so blind that you cannot see how can it be? As I ask even myself how one like me, not highly educated or well-traveled, no college degree in biology or chemistry, but the simplicity in which atrocities are committed against *each other because of nationality, color, or looks is truly disgusting to behold. So, as I have said before, whether you believe in creation, God, or a higher power, which I myself believe in God and his son, who I accept as my Lord and Savior and who died for my sins, so that I may be forgiven, as you progress with science and tech, and search for life afar in the stars above and yet to find any sign. My own opinion and belief are that there is plenty you just do not know exactly what to look for, How or where, but such a complex design and balance of what is needed for life to form and exist here, where we stay is proof enough for me of his existence.*

That is the only display I need to know even though I have had more than you can imagine proving to me of his infinite mercy, love, and wisdom. Some would argue needing some concrete logical proof and probably still would not believe. You will not deceive me. I need no such display as my faith and experience and belief are enough, and he has gifted me with his spirit. And as I nurture and grow in it, I am forever thankful and grateful to our Creator in heaven and our Savior. But also, the complexity and need of ecological balance with nature for survival of everything man or beast is even more proof of intelligent design and not chance the need for perfect placement of our world to our sun for life to survive and thrive the need for the right amount of chemical interaction to produce the air, we breathe or to have rain, snow, and sleet; the rotation needed for gravity that keeps you firmly on the ground you walk on. Even the design of something is as simple as a leaf on the tree, with its veins and the function of trees to create oxygen. The complexity of it all is proof enough, I say, once again of design and not the big bang, which would mean everything is here by chance and luck!

Even more absurd to me let me try to explain how I see it. For me to believe what I do whether true or not I gain everything and lose nothing. Not only do I become a better person by showing compassion for others and trying to uplift ... In the Endgame when the time comes believing as I do looking forward to Eternity with our creator while if you choose to live for just the here and now only for self in this brief span of life we live on the if you are wrong and there is more to it than just the here and now you lose everything ... for a minute's pleasure. When in truth life for all could be so much more if we get it together here and after. Again, this Division we cause and divide ourselves into factions, fractions of what we could be as a whole so much more could we accomplish its sad that we are in such a disarray I pray that one day we see the light and error of such beliefs as being better than another because of one color or the other.

Who Am I? And What I See

Since my birth on this earth, I have been chasing death with each breath I breathe, bringing me closer to that moment I have at one time been seeking and running hand and hand. but no longer am I seeking escape but to embrace this gift of life that has been given to us all. As I escape this misery you have made for us with your uncaring ways and I praise my Creator and Savior while walking this long and narrow road. I am watching your disregard for life, love, and compassion in all forms and fashions. When you face choices between these, you usually choose greed not from need. As you hide the truth for no other reason than to line your coffers and we suffer as you claim the expense of production outweighs the need there is no other greater need than preserving life as we know it for the moment. I know you hide the fact that you have cure for certain diseases or maladies, but out of greed you choose not to cure but have us endure suffering these afflictions to fill prescription after prescription to support your economy or capitalism keeping us hooked physically, mentally and monetarily. For what

money is there in creating an effective cure when you can continuously get paid for temporary remedies and keep people in pain and suffering, while lining your pockets with cash to fill your coffers with offers of temporary relief in the belief of population cultivation or control when you hold the power to heal but choose to deal in death. Do you really think you will get away and not pay the price for playing with the lives of others, acting like you have the right to decide who lives or dies, telling half-truths full of lies while precious lives are lost? And those that survive are trapped in a sea of agony and despair that cares for none, endlessly struggling against oppressive forces that keep society in a chokehold that slowly strangles the will of its citizens who become as mindless as the drones of a beehive just to survive from 9-to-5, letting emotions grow numb from the steady bombardment of wicked actions seen across the globe becoming desensitized and uncaring at times which make it even easier to commit more atrocious actions as being seen this day and age not just by older but younger and younger generations.. And the faith and fate of humanity is tested through the insanity we suffer. To whose satisfaction are such actions performed while refusing to be deceived by the tricks and lies I see through my very own eyes. I despise such actions of deceit while watching the world grow hotter and colder and seasons interchanging and mixing together to the point of not knowing where one ends and the other begins a sign of the times and our Savior's return.

I have been born into this war-torn society of loosening morals and values, loss of faith and belief. As I hold on to my own belief and love of our Creator and Savior for everything, he has given me thus far, not failing to understand and realize what my eyes have been opened to and what is at hand as the sands of time seem to be quickening, and it truly amazes me to what degree that so many deny or fail to see, and I myself do not ask why as I hear so many cry wondering at the reasons for all that is occurring as I see through the games seeming to sleepwalk but wide awake, and it is a shame it has come to this point.

I am grateful, not hateful to be able to see through the lies and though my mentality may spin as though caught in a whirlwind of despair for how much I care. I do not mind the pain that at times, feels as bad as a migraine as I gain and learn from the ordeal while slowly becoming divergent and remerging and thanking my Savior and Father in heaven for his many blessings and lessons that I have received and continue to receive. I am learning that it allows me to know the tricks being done and played not be easily swayed by hollow words served by a forked tongue, and you act like it's a game. Who is to blame? Go a few pages back and remind yourself as I often do the same It really is a shame as I myself have awakened as if from a spell or deep slumber to be torn between decisions of where shall I begin to make my incision like a surgeon, purging this cancerous disease eating away at society and the world today the games we play with each other using people like pawns on a chess board. As I pray for a way and a better day, I hope I don't have to make you pay for the way you play games of the mind using trickery and deceit half-truths seeming true knowing exactly what you do or try to undue.

I have been blessed by the Most High My Adonai, My Elohim/YHWH names once used but removed and replaced as I try to address these issues and begin to use my gift that I have been given and show my face in this place finding my position in this life. I have tried time and again to reason or reach out with no doubt in my mind, but understand as I land another blow and grow through the trials and tribulations and games we play, I say to one and all as I stand tall and have done no whining or complaining while slowly climbing from the bottom to the top of the pile. It's my turn you have grown fat while so many have starved as I grab these reigns and take hold, beginning to carve out a slice of the so-called American dream a half-truth told by the elite to placate the masses while the struggle is real trying to deal with the hurdles put in place that dictate race relations causing them to sour by the hour whether because of affirmative action which does not make up for 400 years of miseducation, slavery and segregation combined in just 60years. Let's be real as we still deal with ignorance and racism biased opinions all around the globe... trying not to let my warm heart grow cold as I mold these words that need to be heard and served them on a platter watching your lies shatter like glass before my very eyes as I see such hypocrisy. What games are you playing as I look around, gaining ground and checking my surroundings. Gaining traction watching factions stay divided because of lies told visually thru your TV.

    I have much to say, but which way to go as I watch some stare and smirk like they think they are better or above me because of the color of their skin and have the right to judge, yet I smile, staying in stride, thanking my Father in heaven and my Lord and Savio the only reason I am able to mind my behavior and not lay you down on the ground face first as I open up and let you know you need to be very very careful I'm hunting devils and snakes, pay attention to his coming in these last days watching the wicked ways of humankind that's not so kind.

This I know and believe it or not as I watch Salem's lot grow hot and the plot thickens, there is no chicken here or scaredy cat nor fat rat but A child of the one true LIVING GOD My Adonai/YHWH/Elohim/Jehovah.

Don't make me act a fool or out of place. You know the rules as well, as I, and I choose to win and not lose. As I cruise through this life, watching the world spin in rotation wondering about its foundation built on sand getting out of hand or on rock taking stock in the creator of creation while looking for my queen worthy of this king. Escaping the misery at my victory. Watching history unfold through eyes half closed but wide awake. If I catch a snake in my midst, his head I will crush with my heel as I praise my Lord in heaven for the seven's he has embedded in me in my mind, body, and soul, while rolling through this world that has gone astray and lost its way.

As I speak out of this feeling growing inside of me, so many try to doubt or disillusion me. There will be no intrusion or confusion, it is not a game or charade as so many put up a façade hiding who they truly are as I give praise to the Most High. There is no lie. You can feel it or see it in my eyes as I wise up and rise from the ashes like a phoenix to be reborn.

Some have trash-talked behind my back and used abusive words on me to varying degree and I have let it slide of my shoulder like oil and water not mixing, but as I use this gift and lift my head up and say in more ways than one that he has blessed me with his holy spirit. I have turned my cheek week after week not seeking retribution or vengeance, but not meek or weak, not an entertainer or dancer, but gifted in more ways than one. Giving All praise to him, who is our Creator and my Lord and Savior. My behavior may be wild at times, yet mild as I smile, thinking of things you can't imagine nor fathom what I have experienced or seen. Not just dreams of getting money, and my queen, but schemes to end the screams of pain and agony of the many that suffer with no relief to have received such a gift to uplift as I lift up my head and say to this feeling even though some may disbelieve or say no.

> *I know from the signs I have seen, felt, and from the reactions of many and not just a few, it is true and not a ruse, and I chose not to abuse or misuse that which has been given, and I am thankful for the blessing, He has given me and as I learn to appreciate and nurture and not destroy the joy, I feel at what is growing within me. Even through all the doubt the jesting and the way some try to test. As I gauge reactions and see fractions of what truly could be, how can you wonder, why, when you try to twist and turn and try to steal or take what he has given me or another instead of doing the same to get your own, which is not for sale or to be given away as I make my way through it all. If you even have a clue, then what is it you try to do? Have me misconstrued, misjudged or screwed? You will pay the price, not me, for such actions as he is watching not just through me and my eyes, but your own. But I have shown compassion during atrocious actions. I chose to try and give you a hand to understand as time*

is running out no doubt in my mind as I find my way through this mess being blessed, watching what each one is doing. Life is not a game. It is a shame you play as such, using and abusing each other over color, race, and breed, letting greed, jealousy, and envy take seed, keeping us from being more from shore to shore as wars and famine rage like wildfires blazing. Turn the page as I stage my entry gently, praying that you open your eyes to our demise. That I see with no surprise the lies being told to hold fleeting power as nations rise and fall and all get caught in this melting pot that grows so hot that it is boiling over as the seasons mix together, not of the norm, and a storm is brewing while screwing creation our station to be caretakers, not destroyers, claiming to be grown but through my eyes I see children doing tit for tat this for that wasting precious time and lives. I am in no way perfect. I have my own sins, scars, and faults and am thankful to our Creator that he sent us hi son a Savior so I may be forgiven for living this way, not only from within, but without with no doubt I have accepted my Creator and Lord and Savior as my King and Maker, so not a faker, but caretaker from what I have been seen been given and felt as I have knelt and prayed day after day and continue to do so.

A new age is dawning as I yawn and stretch, but the wretched shape I see forming before me. In this war-torn world, as I take a hold and mold these words like clay with compassion and start to rebuild while wielding these words like a sword, they say the pen is mightier. from being falsely accused, misused, and abused in one way or another to being my brother's keeper, as I use this gift I have been given in a different manner than most, raising the banner of our Lord and Creator high in the sky, coming from a checkered past as I blast through the lies and deception at a mixed reception, cleaning my act while gleaning facts and remaining true to my Creator and Savior through these dark times of loose morals and lost values, I have minded my behavior to a degree, not a pimp or player, a truth Sayer, and lie slayer. And you dare compare as I stare, I care at times more than I should, while roaming through these streets, misunderstood at times, taken for granted while eyes slanted, and feet planted firmly on the ground, nurturing the seed planted within me by our Creator, not a hater or faker, but caretaker, as I thank our maker for giving me this blessing and yearning for more as I adore my true calling and not falling for your games.

As I tame my own anger for such actions that shame you and me, slowly taking flight with no fright as I fight back the urges of animosity or hate and negate the feelings of needing revenge that hinge on the edge of payback for the way you think you can play your game. Placing trust in him who has blessed me with the spirit and thanking him for the sevens embedded in me. Don't make me break you in two for the things you do. I caught you playing and I'm praying I don't have to hurt you in any way as I cherish the gift of life, he has given me as should you, that which you have no right to harm in any form or fashion as I switch gears, saying no fear of any you here. only of our Father in heaven and his judgement if I should go astray, he who has the right to judge not only flesh but also mind, body, and soul that is whom you should fear as the time draws near. as I roll through this life watching strife and wicked actions committed all around, watching the signs of the times, knowing I am growing, and he is returning while yearning for more in this life as well as the next. You who need to understand this land and this world that has fallen and became the playground of Demons and Devils. This is the proving ground your chance to prove your worth and where your soul shall reside when the time comes and it's all over will you be forever lost or forever in his presence and grace.

> *And I say, Father, forgive me for my sinful way's past, present and future as I always give him praise for sending his son who I accept as my Lord and Savior. so that I may be forgiven and be given eternal life to be in his presence and an ear at his side as I have been balling out of control in the past but getting a grip at last as I dip thru these city streets, watching and observing while serving our Lord and Creator however I can, I can't continue to watch things get so out of hand as man, woman, and child continue to abuse and misuse each other in such a way that is abhorrent in the eyes of our Creator, who is greater than all, the dismay I feel while we fall into such a disarray. I pray that we find our way back to his arms before our world is torn asunder, and we blunder the wonder of his creation facing total annihilation for the violations we commit toward him and each other for personal gain, the pain we inflict as some continuously perpetuate such actions, do as though wilt are you serious? So, shall it be done unto you, the atrocity that you commit tenfold unfold upon you and your whole ilk down generation after generation, the sorrow, the agony, the pain be done unto you and yours is what you would have? Be very careful, very careful in these final hours.*

Where do I begin as I start to realize that seeing is believing and how deceiving things have been visually demoralizing and demeaning. The way you portray things in a light to sway people away from the hidden agenda of the so-called secret elite, but as it has been written, the truth remains in plain sight for those that seek it. The time is coming for an end to this game that has been played. As I myself begin to lay bare the facts, I have gleaned to be true. Let me be sure that you understand what I am saying as I have been praying for a way to escape the misery I see before me.

> *As I have been awakened to such a sight, as wars continue raging the staging for final confrontation, demonstrations of ill will as well as good in and out, the hood worldwide in every nation and its foundation. As the world and people cry out for our Saviors grace and fast return, the behavior I am witnessing is astounding in many ways as the day's rays of sunshine come and go and the world is in throws of a change as it has been preordained as I reign blow after blow of my own as we reap what has been sown and things have grown out of hand. Where do you stand as we are on the edge of this ledge to whom do you pledge your allegiance Creator or Destroyer? As we are all one but Different variations in each nation. Foundations built upon sand, grand empires rising and falling, with appalling behaviors toward neighbors alike! Whether slanted eyed or round as I tear down brick after brick of trickery.*

Whether blue-eyed, brown or green, whatever shade or grade. Whether light skinned or dark skinned we are one we are humankind made in our creator's image learn to act accordingly. As the world spins on its axis and we track this life back age after age and you turn the page of these chapters, the laughter of masters and the tears of slaves, and I brave this new era to erase the terror, the bearer of news as I choose not to lose. The clues I have followed, honey-coated words filled with lies, I refuse to swallow while we wallow in Satan's hollow. Many would ask who is to blame. How is it when something bad happens, we blame the devil, or ask God why he let this happen? Do we not understand the gift that was given? To which road you should take or what path to follow? If everything was predestined, then what good would the gift of free will be? The reason being he sees and knows all, but we don't so in his eyes it has been predestined or preordained.

> *We would be nothing more than an automaton or robot. Nothing more than a simple computer program like in the matrix, dutifully following only that which we were programmed to do, not the sentient life/beings we are or were created to be. Or the chance to be forgiven for living the way we have been living. As for asking God why he let this happen. God did not make us to control our actions but has given us guidelines and commandments. We do what we do to ourselves. Being faithless nonbelievers, wayward sinful children, and simply not caring about the actions we commit towards each other and ourselves, we have had many teachers and teachings.*

Living and written examples, of how we should act or treat each other, but it seems we refuse to listen or pay attention to the signs we have been given, and as for the devil, the only power he holds over you, me, we or us is the lies you listen to and choose to ignore or believe in. And that power which you let him have by letting him mislead you into actions to go against what teachings and examples our Creator has shown us to live by. It is your choice, your decision, a gift that has been given. Not to be forced or controlled but to have the chance and option to choose for ourselves what road we take and mistakes we make lake of fire or eternal salvation.

> *And to be forgiven for wrong decisions and actions, if we choose to ask! Since the death of our Savior, the Messiah, our King and Lord. if we wish to change, ask, and accept the sacrifice that has been made for us to fall under grace and not the law. So again, it is we, who allow this to happen to us. It is we who choose to be, but in the end, it is our Creator who will judge us, not you or me with our bias opinions of each other. It is we, as humans, who do this to each other with our lack of respect for life and concern for each other's well- being and me myself. I believe this is just the beginning part of life in which we live where my actions here and now determine what happens in the hereafter after this is over and we leave this plane of existence since I myself believe that this is not all there is and that this is only the beginning to the life that my Creator has breathed into me and has blessed me with to be a part of him and his creation my station to create, not destroy. As I journey through this life, strife with war, whether visual, physical or mental from within to without, there is no doubt in my mind as I find my way. I have prayed continuously for release of the pain as I begin to seize hold and mold these words like a potter molding clay, this game I see played, whether as if like chess or checkers playing people like pawns pieces to be pushed this way and that for one's own amusement or gain. As I yawn and stretch the wretched sight, I am seeing not believing that it has come to this but receiving such a blessing, learning my lessons day in and out, and doing my own walkabout while we talk about the ins and outs of this life. Will we ever learn how not to burn as the world turns on its axis*

revolving around our life-giving sun day after day? The fact is what makes you feel that you can do what you choose and never lose? To abuse and misuse each other the way we do not only killing ourselves but the planet we live on as well. Do you really believe after this there is nothing else? That we are here by chance and there is no meaning? This world teeming with life and the universe our earth exists in. It is known that all will hear and see but few will listen and believe. So, deceive yourself if you will, but you will not deceive me. What will it take to shake loose of evil's grip as our world slips ever closer to Armageddon, the final setting, never forgetting what? my Adonai/Elohim and Lord have done for me, slowly breaking free of the mental and physical chains that hand me bound and blind. Link by link loop by loop while putting God's together armor chink by chink. In these last days, watching mankind's wicked ways unfold before my eyes, as I rise from shattered broken pieces that were scattered about slowly put back together piece by piece, it ceases to amaze me anymore and there is no surprise to our demise as I surmise the damage being done from us, who are his children, made in his image the killing I am seeing being done like it's a norm this storm that is brewing.

Such a waste of precious life, and we hasten our own demise with the construction of weapons of mass destruction. What will it take for us to wake as a whole and make a difference, looking for deliverance from up high while so many die for the wicked state of life we live caused by our own actions, wandering the earth lost and unforgiving, reliving sins from past to present in a seemingly endless cycle of sadness and madness that needs to be broken. I am hoping to reach out with these words that I hope are heard as I serve it on a platter to shatter the lies holding the wool over the eyes of so many. Can we break free of this never-ending cycle I see before me as we hold the power in this dark hour from our Creator to be greater than what we have been to this day? I pray as we have strayed far from his grace in this place, if we do not change, it has been preordained, the pain with no gain from the times of our forefathers to the life as we know it now will end in fire as we are consumed by our desires maddened by a lust for power consumed by hate showing no concern for the fate of ourselves, others, children, siblings, or sires.

No idols or Engraven images saeth Our Creator Adonai/ YHWH so what concern is it of the color or race of our messiah as We visually have been deceived from the paintings that have become like idols to so many. what should be important is the message and way of life he taught the pain he went through to show his love for us and we continue to disregard, abuse and misuse each other showing lack of respect for our women and children in all walks of life, who is more precious than a child unknowing and guiltless in the eyes of our Creator? To you and me, they look for guidance and do we teach them love or hate as we wait for the return of our Savior? What fate do we leave them with a world full of animosity, hate, racial and facial discrimination what foundation do we build, as we visually, physically, and mentally assault each other, it seems so out of hand that things gotten and rotten to the core as the only cure is Agape Love.

Have we forgotten the teachings of love and compassion wondering why it's so easy for our children to commit these heinous murderous rampages being done all over the country in schools and elsewhere taking and mimicking the adults they see and learn from with all of your hatred and anger that you display the dismay I feel to be around or associated with any that are so ignorant to think they are better than another for any reason? while I fashion this blade for this war of the words and minds. While others fashion weapons of war for mass destruction and corruption runs rampart through the highest positions in world governments across the globe and we hold these truths to be self-evident (of what?) and presidents take residencies, causing calamities across the globe, clashing with each other as innocent casualties pile up, will we continue upon this path, earning the wrath of our maker, as nature and creation alike suffer from the blows and the world is in the throes of woes from those actions? And we are supposed to be caretakers of creation? But facing annihilation for violations committed with no remorse for the course we follow. I hear so many.

Words, but most seem hollow. I can no longer swallow lies so easily told in a world that's so cold.

As I begin to hold up my head, looking through these eyes, as I rise and wise up. As my mind begins to clear and the years seem to pass with the blinking of an eye and I try to make sense of it all. Slowly arriving, surviving, and growing, knowing something is wrong with this picture I see. Surrounded in a sea of animosity causing me to wonder why man could so easily blunder and plunder the wonder of creation. Our station to have dominion, in my opinion, is a blessing we continually misuse and abuse, taking for granted the power and gift we have been given. Do we really deserve to be forgiven for this living and how effortlessly we waste life that is more precious than money and gold or than anything we hold dearer as it becomes ever so clear? But such is the way of our true Creator and his love and compassion for us, his children, for us to be forgiven. And we continue the killing of each other because of color, greed, and lust. To what end can you justify such actions? And you would claim to be chosen or better? As I type each letter, because of what reason are such treasonous actions are committed? And the terror you cause by the error of your ways? And how you use visualization and manipulation of words to confuse facts to cause acts of such degradation in each nation? Are you having fun? *When it's all done, do you think you can run to outer space and find a place to hide? When his spirit resides in everything he has made, there is nowhere you can go, or nothing you can do that he does not know as you show exactly where your allegiance lies as I begin to tie the loose ends together and tether such a tie that binds one another who are brother, sister, father, mother, daughter and son alike, and so on down the line. The time is coming. The vibe is vibrating. The trumpet is playing, and I myself am hearing as we are nearing an age. The stage is being set. The marionettes are dancing as the puppet masters are pulling their strings and things are being brought into the light that was once in the dark. And I come to my own realization and begin to play my position using the gift I have been given by our Creator who is greater than all, and I begin to stand up tall, appalled at what I am bearing witness to. You, me, and we are in this together to the very bitter end. As I try to mend broken bridges between races, different faces, and variations of one nation under God, this civilization as we call it. Where is the civility in the brutality and casualties of our wars? So, before it's all over and I'm in and out because there is no doubt, I have been waiting to roll out since the day I was born that fateful morn, mind torn with thoughts that could consume my very being lost in a world ruled by greed fed and consumed by lies that fly easily from the tip of the tongue, wanting me to believe a nation of equality under God but refusing to be deceived as I watch many families grieve as their children bleed and greed has this nation and many more muddled in foreign affairs while its own foundation crumbles from within, hearing the cries while my eyes open, hoping it's not too late as I wake and realize how far we all have fallen. Taking for granted the gift we have been given, and we continue live apart from his grace. Will He not embrace all that face their sins and ask for forgiveness? Can we all that believe not trace each and every race back to the tower of Babel and Cain and Abel the very story that split us into fractions factions of what we once were before we chose to reach too far and be scarred in such a way that unto this day we still are sundered? Have we forgotten and become so rotten with greed that we no longer pay heed to what is written in stone? Once again, thinking we are grown and all I am seeing is children with malicious toys of destruction easily destroying the gift of life are we so fallen that we cause all this strife with no remorse for the course that is chosen; claiming to have come so far, yet regressing back to barbaric actions. To whose satisfaction do we continue such a degree of animosity. For what reason do we commit such a treason to each other? Whether you believe in evolution or creation, the relation is undeniable from Adam and Eve if you believe in creation. To the smallest entity of the belief in evolution is the only solution to the pollution of our souls is to die for the way we lie, steal, kill and deal poorly with each other. Have we not learned to play with fire, is to be burned, do we not have the power of choice, is this what you want? What we choose to be? So, like it was written in the beginning with this knowledge of good and evil, thou shalt surely die and we have the nerve to wonder why it is so? When we know right from wrong but regularly chose the latter do, we even understand all that our world has to offer from the darkest crevice to the deepest ocean and we reach for the stars not knowing or learning how to heal our hidden wounds racing to destruction with the construction of weapons of war. Brilliant minds wasted on wicked thoughts and actions. What if all your knowledge, time and skill was spent with better intent could we not heal the sick, feed the hungry house the homeless? And eventually populate the very stars you wish and dream under, instead of blundering and plundering the wonder of creation and this life and planet where we live? Just food for thought that I believe our God has blessed me to feel and say. God's Blessing and Love to all who are his children and my family.*

Speaking Out

So as I begin to speak out, no doubt in my mind while watching the signs of the times with the seasons intermixing, not missing my cue as you continue to treat life like a game of chess, using pawns against pawns, testing the emotional waters of our world and tempers flare ever hotter, we hang on the edge of destruction because of the games you play with lives that are not yours to abuse instead of looking for cures like Louie pastor you choose to cause cancerous disease for basic needs to feed your greed, but I have found a way to pay you back for how you act and to ease my pain and gain a hold while loosening your grip by molding these words like clay in the hands of a master artisan at work, thanking my Creator in heaven for the sevens embedded in my brain and soul, waiting to rollout while traveling through life at a speed trying to pay heed to what is written in stone because I have grown and not your child, even though at times I act wild and rather mild at either end of the spectrum like a pendulum swinging slowly at first then from one extreme to the next, *while you constrict me with your laws and lies, trying to bind me like the snake that you are with your restrictions on my freedom.*

It never ceases to amaze me, refusing to let you phase me as my God has made me, not a product of any man-made theory. Hear me as I thank him for his grace, for the place and life he has given me with the gift to compose pieces of art like Mozart but formulated in words that need to be heard, showing my heart as I do my part, starting in motion slowly like waves in an ocean turning into a full blown tsunami for what I crave to never be a slave in this madness you call civilization a foundation built on the back of others blood sweat n tears, having the nerve to accuse others of savagery and being uncivilized when history tells otherwise if truly read and understood what you and your ancestor have done throughout the centuries and dark ages. I will be free of the lies and misery you cause with your atrocious actions that makes this blessing of life a living hell as you label everything for sale even that which you don't own taken by force and the course you plot is clear as we near the final hour. You will see no fear when looking into my eyes you might find a fire slowing burning and growing. for I try every day to make peace with my Creator to be sure of my place in the cosmic scheme of things in this life and after. squandering the joys with wicked ploys, toys, and abuse. Ahh, the misuse of what is precious.

To what means do we demean ourselves who are supposed to be in his image? You would say to yourself, not me, do not lie, you only kid yourself as I know of my own accord, I fall short of his grace. But make it my place to forever be indebted and ask for forgiveness and grace that I live this way in this mess we call life and try to change my actions for the better of myself and other fellow human beings as we are of one breed one race humanity and one fateful deed causes us to fall to this greed and obsession with power when we have no right to control each other's lives when we can't even control our own selves. Who am I and who are you to say what is good for me? If you think you can, then should I not also think that I can tell you what is good for you? I am not your child and you are not mine, but we are kin, whether you accept it or not. As I said before, you only lie to yourself. I refuse to kid myself or to lie to you. Realize what you do and how far we have fallen. We could be so much more, but yet we fail miserably so badly by this savagery that we commit in each city, nation, and village every day in so many ways with no hesitation. To pillage and plunder because you can? Such nonsense knowing that you would not appreciate such deeds committed against you or yours in return an eye for an eye so should I begin a rampage and payback in kind every slight every innuendo that has been done but as I hold fast my anger, as we are the ones to blame not God or the devil.

We as humans, who have been given freedom of choice, and we make these stupid choices and wrong decisions to treat each other as inconsequential and meaningless when all have meaning and positions to play in this life that is not to be taking for a game or granted. We have barely even scratched the surface of this that we call living, and I fear we will not get far on this road that we travel as I begin to unravel and travel far and wide not to hide this feeling inside. And I begin growing and showing, knowing what is right and what is wrong, while these words start flowing, throwing my all in this gift. To lift, not put down or step on those that need to be assisted, coming around to my senses in these last days. As games are run to manipulate and violate each other who are brother, mother, sister, father, son, and alike, white, yellow, or black as we attack each other for ignorant reasons whether of greed or racism the hatred of another because of their color how ignorant and wicked is this? To hate not because of someone committing an offensive action but because of simple color. Hatred period is a strong emotion that can overpower the sensible thoughts and actions, the fact remains that the pains and the stains being caused by the games we play with each other to smother one's dreams, whether the screams are heard in the middle of night or broad daylight.

> *As I lock and Load and take stock, not in a weapon, but in my Adonai and Savior while using rhyme and reason in time as I shine and take time, not hitting rewind but pressing forward, taking faith as small as a mustard seed and letting it grow., the ridicule, and visual abuse, the misuse of simple actions down to the smallest vibration striations from in a whirlwind of sanctions causing tumultuous results, and while many are anxiously waiting our Savior's return as I yearn to be free of these disastrous things I see occurring, it's not a mystery, as we go through history, finding facts and traces of ancient civilizations, seeing faces from our past, what stasis are we in from atoms to Adam and Eve so on this Eve, as I receive my own blessings, the lessons we learn as the world turns on its axis, facts and non-fiction, the tables and the stories Cain or Abel, the blood that is shed by all is red as we tread down this path, do we laugh at the wrath or sigh in relief of the belief of the second coming. I am wondering of the*

rapture as I capture your state of mind, can you relate as we wait for the return of our Creator the things I bring to bear as we stare of into the future. Yes, I care, do you? as I stare, weary-eyed, we have come to a point, a. As we are at the edge of this ledge. Red, white, yellow, or black!

The facts that I track back to the beginning of time in this rhyme as things seem to remain the same even regressing to varying degrees, the shame as many want to claim they are gods, kings or queens as I nock this arrow in my bow and take aim, such claims and actions shown are far from the claims as the flames of war burn from little embers into roaring flames, are we lost to the point of no return as I yearn to learn more of the truth rather than following lies that try to keep us in a state of confusion and continuing conflict whether internal or external. What about you and me can we come together and be what we are meant to become as his creation and children made in his image. as I lend my hand into this mess. The stress and frustration as I begin to address issues that I see close to home and abroad and I nod to you and the things we go through so similar yet so different as we feel the same pain or sorrow. What a mess while being blessed while through this looking glass eye look, not Alice in wonderland, but humanity how you blunder as I thunder and lay blow after blow for what do you know? As we go through the ages, the stages of life! Truly what is known other than one's own experiences and lessons taught by elders what truly do we know and understand from our land or past histories of conflict and war have not learned how the actions we make or take as we rape this world of its resources from horses to whales and some species become extinct, the gales of wind blows the throes and the woes of gigantic tsunamis from volcanic eruptions to corruption from global warming and changing weather patterns to brush fires and wildfires alike, we, who are akin while the earth spins and gravity keeps us terra firm from the worm to the fly, as we try to coexist. We mix and mingle, as I light a single flare! Beware as my own eye's focus, and I begin to pinpoint each, and every action has its own reaction from contraction to the constriction of contraptions this caption as I write this small fellow so mellow and begin to bellow out come about don't be foolhardy. As the signs have just begun, trumpets are sounding with a resounding ring, are you caring as I begin bearing down. Not playing, but I'm saying it to one and all. Atheist/Christian/ Muslim/Jew are you a believer or not.

Spiritualist/newage/Buddha/Kemet/Scientologist, whatever your belief system and whoever you are this world we live on we all are one. The atrocities committed city by city, nation upon nation. What is this that we do, you, me, we as we go through life, searching for meaning, looking from within or to the stars from bars and cars driving endlessly in search of the unknown to what point are we arriving, some starving, others carving out their own mark as I spark this ignition on my own mission, wishing upon a star close yet far away. I pray the day comes sooner than later as tempers flare on either side of the equator that we get it together before it's too late as the hourglass sands trickle down can we as humankind turn around and do an about face! Not to erase but replace past transgressions with benevolent actions instead of ignoring the fact that what we have done still haunts us to this day and to say lessons learned and earn our place on this earth a rebirth of a sorts, not a hearse or a curse, let's not go in reverse! As we live and breathe on this earth and learn to traverse this universe, will we be a burden like virus as we consume resources without a care a plague upon the world which serves as our home yet we continue to ignore the signs of how we waste with the haste we take as I refuse to be vague.

The way we act thus far, as if nothing else matters, other than money and power over others manipulating, violating, and annihilating each other as a way of living instead of giving, caring, sharing to have one staring down the barrel of a gun. To be a menace as I condemn this way of acting which is atrocious in nature.

This thinking of being a gangster, nay I say a prankster, hiding behind weapons that threatens one's existence. Pistol-packing punks, dare I say, claiming to be men or women but in truth acting like spoiled children throwing a tantrum but one that is destroying lives that can't be undone.

Needing brute force and weapons to enforce your will. As I deal this blow among many more to come, how uncanny as many fall to so few that choose to act this way, and you cause many a mother, father, brother, and sister to cry as not only children are lost to this rampage but any age is suffering due to the lack of compassion being taught and the new mantra is it's all about me and my wants while it's ok to be concerned about self but when it causes you to affect another because of your greed and ignorance then it becomes an issue. As I try to explain and refrain from being abusive, but such coarse corrosive attitudes at every level of latitude and longitude every angle as many get tangled in such a web of destruction and deceit, with no relief in sight, what a blight, what a plight to be in.

What does it take for you to understand that racism or hatred in any form is born of your ignorance and lack of knowledge? You, who would believe that you are better than another because of color of skin or nationality, what reason do you think this are? What action can you do that cannot be done by another? With the same knowledge or training? This sickness that you suffer to gain enjoyment out of the humiliation and degradation of another. The false sense of power you need because your own life and destiny is out of control or context.

I find it interesting that when you are put through the same pain and trials. It is no longer fun or enjoyable, but despicable and deplorable. So how could you possibly think you are any better than the next? Don't waste your life in a lie full of hate being brainwashed and lost when your life could be spent better achieving greater goals for the good of humanity and escape the insanity of such vane way of thinking and downfall of humanity and to find the true meaning in actions of compassion and understanding. To make better the world we struggle to live in. If you spent such energy, maybe you could discover the answer to longevity or even interstellar travel. There is no limit to what could be achieved, if you took the time to focus on what is truly important. Hate and anger are wasted emotions that are a big part of what leads us down the road to destruction.

> *And if we do not get control of such detrimental emotions, then surely, we have and will fail to be the best that we can ever hope to be or achieve, wasting what little bit of brainpower we use, failing miserably to ascend to a higher state that we were meant for, being made in his image. But our actions continue to make us less, and we remain*

factions and fractions of what we were meant, separated and divided by lies spread across the globe, whether visually or verbally assaulted through the ages as the spiritual war rages and you turn the pages of this book. Hook, line and sinker, this deep thinker that I have become, following a trail of breadcrumbs, to come to this conclusion, refusing the abusing bombardment of apparitions and superstitions alike, banishing my own demons, sending them screaming, steaming, and teeming with fear as I eradicate and annihilate abhorrent thoughts within the deepest darkest crevices of my own mind and find the light to write these words that need to be heard and served as I believe in his word and the truth of his law as well as his grace to take my place as I trace my own lineage back to the motherland of whence we all came, no feeling of shame, not pointing a finger of blame, but as I tame rampart thoughts that whirl through my brain and train to take aim as I fire volley after volley and round after round to pound and grind down trickery of imagery meant to have me bent, and I lend my own cry to this outrageous façade or charade as many parade around, claiming while looting, shooting, and hooting, I have been vibrating and waiting while others gyrating for my turn as I learn to release this pent-up frustration for violations I see, causing this misery to be.

As I free my mind and take flight as I write, thanking our Creator and my Savior for this blessing and lessons I leant as I grow older, my words ever bolder and I shoulder not a burden but don a crown of king and bring to bear this gift and try to uplift and mend rifts that drift so far apart, we are one under the sun/son on this earth that we live. And I give praise to our Creator who is greater than all! Thanking him for my Savior, the only reason I mind my behavior… the perfect love, the perfect gift, the perfect role model, or idol, but not the images or paintings we see; for it is said in the law, no engraven idols or images shall ye worship but the essence of his presence and the message he came to give that we live in harmony and peace with all of creation our station. And these violations committed in each nation, the wasting and debasing of life no matter the color, nationality, or breed. Such a waste of precious life, the gift we have been given to be living and the possibility of being forgiven for living life, man or wife taking life for granted with every breath we breathe like the leaves of a tree life, giving process the balancing act of symbiosis in eco living the giving and taking while making our way. I pray for clear way each and every day as the years fly in and out seemingly ever faster and the seasons seem to linger ever longer and this feeling grows stronger while watching every reaction and interaction from factions or fraction to whose satisfaction are these actions committed to be split apart down the middle, causing a division and confusing to be abusing and using refusing to change. As I arrange and reorder these pieces of this puzzle to paint a picture not perfect but dissect this disorder and pinpoint the issues at hand as I believe our Savior is returning soon whether people believe it or not with everything going on as of date and we wait, would hate for you to be left behind as I try to remind you all as spring lingers into summer and summer into fall and fall into winter into Spring a reminder to be kinder to one and all.

Acceptance

Sometimes, it is hard to accept when things change especially if it's always been your way or only about you. Trust me there will be days in your life when it all seems to twist and turn, and you yearn for that silver lining. When those gloomy days have you down, try to realize you are not alone and when things seem the worst and your life feels cursed instead of blessed and life has you stressed, take a minute, clear your mind, find solace in prayer knowing it will be heard by our Adonai Our Elohim. It may not be answered when you want it, but it has always been when you need it the most. As is the will and way of the highest God of Israel. Even though I may have failed him at times, he has never failed me, and I have never given up but have dusted myself and gotten back up. Be true to yourself and him and He will be true to you. Learn acceptance for the things you cannot change and to change the things you are able. Life might be easier and less full of grief and you may find relief in your belief and higher power if you stand strong and hold on.

Learning when to let things go, and show compassion after a fashion not letting it get out of hand but to understand that you can make a change for the better or a difference in someone's life other than your own even the littlest thing could be major for someone else, like a simple genuine smile while someone is down may change their frown. A simple hello and a well meant how are you today if you try some may ask why, even try. How would you feel if you were facing a situation that could be avoided and something could have been done but nothing was done for you? To feel alone as if no one cares when a simple act of compassion could save another's life with little effort.

Friends

So many associates, few friends as my amazement never ends watching friends and associates alike take advantage of another for personal gain if given the chance. And so, called friends that in the end are jealous of what you have or are trying to achieve whether monetarily or in a personal fashion. A true friend will always be there and respect you, your values and relationship they will never try and destroy what you are building with another if they truly care and want nothing more than your happiness, you need to learn who that is and not fall for the trickery that will cause misery in your life and relationships personal or otherwise, as so many have built a façade over the years to play the only game, they know how do not allow this to be in your life. But when the tables are turned, they feel spurned and wonder why? Others play the same game and others smile enjoying the pain and sorrow they cause. When a true friend would see you through your time of need, paying heed to your emotional pain, lifting you up when you are down and turning your frown into a smile. Always *by your side, won't hide when you're wrong or right let you know on sight. Won't lie or cheat but treat you with honor and respect. Through the trials and tribulations that life brings to bare, a true friend whether physically or mentally, there you can count on them to be around in your time of need, sharing in the precious moments of your life that one savors without being a burden or taking advantage of you and your situations for their own personal agenda or gain as misery loves company one who is not a true friend can be an affliction bringing you down when you're up tripping you up to fall to their level. So, watch who you're with who you're claiming as your friends in the end their actions and words serve to let you know who they exactly are stand strong when the days seem too long to bare and care for each other who are precious in his eye made in his Image Humanity not one color but Through All Walks of Life and Varying Degree. and realize your value while you live this life that is a blessing and a lesson to be learned.*

Misery

*T*hey say misery loves company which has been shown day after day remember you reap what you have sown saying your grown but acting like a child when things don't go your way throwing a tantrum claiming life isn't fair while preying on others weakness or situations to make yourself feel better or justified. As I pray for better days while watching the ways of mankind in these final days trying to find meaning amongst the madness surrounded by sadness from seemingly impossible situations, glad this gift of life has been given to me slowly escaping the misery that tries to surround and pound me down to the ground holding my head high while praising the most high Adonai My God of Israel. Seeking forgiveness from him for my sinful ways while thanking him for all the days through my life and for sending his Son My Savior/Brother and King, He has always been with me no matter the situation I have been facing only by his grace have I been able to face the trials and misery that wish to see me fail, they pale in comparison to his love, grace and glory so being less than *human or subhuman of not mattering that has been shown throughout history by the treatment of light vs dark skinned and the portrayal as such.*

Racism/White Power

*A*s you cry white power trying to make others cower as you shower words of hate claiming to be better because of your skin tone being pale as you fail miserably with your actions and words of hatred the fact that u can commit such acts of atrocity to humanity itself whether you like it or not we are of one race just different variations of his image in which we ALL are made and put the nail in your own coffin sealing your fate with such hate proving to our creator and the world you are not greater, not civilized but barbaric and wicked with your actions claiming to be chosen but posing by killing his children with no remorse for your ugly deeds your lies are unraveling your time is coming there will be no running this life or the next for the pain you cause with your lies and misplaced hate. You are no better than the next, but your actions are showing that you're less than the rest. And the difference between the cry of black power, black lives matter versus white power is it's not a Mantra for hatred or separation rather of inclusion and fighting the disillusion of being less than *human or subhuman of not mattering that has been shown throughout history by the treatment of light vs dark skinned and the portrayal as such.*

My Queen

My Queen, ever since you came into my life you have bewitched me with your beauty, it is my duty as your king to bring joy into your life in any way that I can ease your fears and wipe away your tears if you are in pain, I will bring you pleasure; I treasure every minute I have been given with you. I am forever yours as I hope you are forever mine, our fates entwined since the beginning of time we let none come between what we build; the world is yours for it has been written in stone, I am forever smitten by your love, above all, except for the most HIGH Adonai. I will always honor you by giving you all of me in every way that I can, never to have you worry if I am true; I am always with you and by your side. My queen, my love, my heart is yours forever more. So, as I walk this fallen world alone at the time till you find your way to me and we become one trusting that no one can break the bond he has given us and allowed us to build. Till the day we leave hand in hand to be with him in eternity. I am yours and you are mine

forever in time words unsaid and never spoken but felt and shown through the way we see each other in our eyes.

The Final Hours

The First trumpets are sounding with a resounding blare! Are you listening? Sounds being heard in the air around the globe Do you even care as wars are raging everywhere overseas and lives are being lost at what cost for whatever reason as the seasons intermix and change at a rapid pace, we face certain destruction with the construction of such weapons of war. While fathers kill sons and sons kill fathers, mothers kill daughters and daughters against daughter as well as brother against brother everywhere over the globe such atrocities I am witnessing in every city down here. And The World Bleeds from deeds done past, present and future staining the ground where bodies are found. While I begin to shine and glisten, I have been listening and watching everything down here. I stand firm giving praise to my holy GOD of Israel My Adonai My Elohim YHWH he is watching and listening to everything going on down here as I beseech my creator who is greater than everything anywhere through this vast universe. Will we heed the call and stand tall while so many fall victims to greed and

various deeds of wickedness? Pay heed to the choices you make in these last days as the wicked ways of humankind come out of the dark into the light in the final hours. I give continuous praise to my creator and Elohim and raise up my head and say I am but clay and he is the master potter that molds me and made in his image at times I may seem as mad as the hatter of Alice in wonderland with my actions and words yet continuously wondering why mankind blunders the wondrous gift given to be forgive while living in this mess to be blessed by such a creator. And at other times to be as crazy as the joker from Gotham looking for his Harley Quinn living in this sinful fallen world. I am born to win sign of the twins created by the most High his willing servant and vassal building my castle brick by brick asking him for my forgiveness as I live this life seeking my queen for, I am king as I bring my gift to bear fruit seeking his continued blessings and protection for family, friends and his children. My GOD, My Creator as I bear witness to such atrocities in every city and every callous action my eyes have been opened, I no longer sleep for so many weep from the injustice being committed by every clan of man some worse than others brothers and fathers, mothers and sisters all in the eyes of our Lord. The trumpets are sounding with a resounding call! Are you listening or do you even care? While on this plain of existence watching everything going on through eyes of a different perception and deception is used to distort and hide the truth. explain what you are doing ruining creation our station to be care takers not makers of doom with a loud boom from my canon while landing blow after blow watching the aftermath and afterglow of wars being raged the stage is being set for Armageddon and the day of judgement there will be no running no hiding not any star as far as the eye can see he is watching and residing everywhere. The First Trumpets are sounding with a resounding blare! Are you listening or do you even care? Sounds being heard in the air around the globe The time is coming for you to decide which side you choose for the choice is yours and has always been, you have been given fore warning while the globe is warming. The warning has been sounded the call has been made a call to arms a call to cease and desist a call to resist the wickedness that invades every thought or action being committed as the atrocities are shown for every eye to see crimes done with no regard to who is harmed. Brother against brother family against family cousin against cousin blood being spilled in the street's day in and day out night after night day after day everywhere in every. As the dust settles and the gloom stretches over the event horizon, it's not surprising battles on land, sea and air the earth is groaning and moaning with such a sound that none can deny some say it is natural some say even musical while others say unearthly and unnatural no matter what is said, the disastrous effect is apparent. Some say it has been foretold what do you think or say? I asked those that have seen and heard, by thine own eyes and ears, what do you think is the meaning of such portent events? I for one think it is a warning for all to be ready for the day that is coming sooner than later, the second advent and coming has been foretold and preordained, you cannot deny what is before your very own eyes if you are open to the truth and it is in you who will see what goes on around you and cannot deny what has been foretold from days long past you have been given clue after clue of what is due and to come but continue to do as you will. Do not be misled for I only display what is already in play, I will not hide or be misled I do not beguile you with minced words but play the cards that I have been dealt and lay them plain for all to see. Pay attention to what goes on around you for you have your own part to play in this game you call life which is not a game as many claim but a test to see who deserves ascension and who deserves descending, the ending to be told by the part you chose to play are you a pawn waiting to be king? Or a king being played as a pawn? Taking the chance of being captured being laid to rest? Or are you truly a king guarded well by your queen and men? For the trumpets have sounded with a resounding blare! Are you listening, do you even care?

The State of Affairs as I See It

The How shall I begin to explain the things I see which not only disturbing but amazing not just the duplicity of the system. But those who interpret and implement its execution I guess it would be easy to begin with your 45th, his whole campaign platform was built on hate, division and perversion of the truth. Let's do a quick comparison, this presidency which has been scandal ridden since the first day with Russian collusion, refusing to quiet hate rhetoric that has arisen. Let's Explore the difference you have a group of people i.e., white nationalist movement Creed White Power, and anyone that doesn't look like or act like them are inferior races to be used or dealt with as of no consequence, then you have Black Lives Matter which from my meager understanding is something simple as pointing out the continuous and systematic mistreatment of people of color in a country that has a shady beginning. How can one even compare the two or any other movement? And as soon as the African American community begins to stand up or speak out you have the those that try and sabotage *or weaken the movement with things like all lives matter etc. Which is a fact but in this country since the beginning has a track record of showing that all lives don't matter or only matter if your Caucasian. And Still to this day show preferential treatment to Caucasian. For example, let's see in most recent events the school shootings:*

- One student was killed and eight others were injured earlier this week in an attack on an English class at STEM School Highlands Ranch. **Two students were apprehended and charged with the shooting**, which took place just miles from Columbine High School, the site of a massacre 20 years ago. 1 Let's see the Jew's and the holocaust death camps,
- A Savannah State University student was shot and HYPERLINK "https://www.wtoc.com/2019/05/07/policerespond-reports-shooting-university-commons/" wounded HYPERLINK "https://www.wtoc.com/2019/05/07/
- police-respond-reports-shooting-university-commons/" in a residential hall on campus. **The authorities said a man who was not a student was arrested in the shooting**.
- Two students were killed, and four others were wounded after a gunman opened fire in an anthropology class at the University of North Carolina at Charlotte. One of the students who was killed, Riley Howell, was credited with charging HYPERLINK "https://www.nytimes.com/2019/05/06/us/ riley-howell-uncc-shooting.html?module=inline" and body-slamming the gunman, stopping the massacre.
- A 17-year-old student at Robert E. Lee High School was shot and wounded in an arm by another student, the police said. **The school was placed on lockdown and the assailant was arrested**. According to news media reports, it was the

second time in two years that a student had taken a gun to that school and shot another student.

In each of these situations An ARMED Individual (Caucasian) was apprehended without killing them...

- (Black)Travon
- **JaQuavion Slaton (Black)** was killed in a hail of as many as 10 shots in Fort Worth, Texas, on June 11, 2019. Officers claimed Slaton had a gun but had not provided any proof.
- **Gregory Hill Jr.** was killed in a matter of seconds after police shot him in his own garage in Fort Pierce, Florida, on Jan. 14, 2014. Reports said residents called police with a noise complaint because of the loud music being played in the garage. When Hill opened the garage and saw it was police, he tried to close it before police shot him in the head and elsewhere. Hill's family has maintained he was unarmed when he was shot.
- On June 6, 2019, **Ryan Twyman (Black)** was reportedly unarmed and shot 37 times by the Los Angeles Sheriff's department.
- On Jan. 22, 21-year-old **Jimmy Atchison (Black)** was shot and killed by police officer Sung Kim. Police allegedly entered an apartment complex with military assault-style rifles to execute a run-of-the- mill warrant for robbery.
- On February 9, 2019, **Willie McCoy (Black)** fell asleep at a drive through in Vallejo, California. When police approached him, he was shot 25 times. Police claimed there was a gun in his lap. His lawyer told The New York Times shortly after the shooting, "He was just riddled with bullets. It was really a shock how many times he was struck."
- **Emantic "EJ" Fitzgerald Bradford Jr. (Black)** was shot by police while trying to save people from a shooter at an Alabama mall. The military veteran was killed on Thanksgiving night.

- • On Jan. 15, the 18-year-old was reportedly attempting to steal a car from a police officer who wasn't in uniform. He reportedly slid into the driver's seat the cop was pumping gas. Griffin tried to drive away and the officer filed multiple shots. There was no weapon on Griffin.
- TO MANY to even continue
- In These situations, UNARMED(Black) were killed by police. And you say All Lives Matter? And then you have your 45th Make America Great Again. When was America Great?
- Slavery? if we use 1619 as the beginning and the 1865 Thirteenth Amendment as its end then it lasted 246 years?
- A Century of Racial Segregation, 1849–1950

So, if anything it should be Make America Great but not with all this hate and continuous miseducation and representation of the facts. So, do we move forward and if so how. First and foremost is the Fact that Slavery Over the period of the Atlantic Slave Trade, from approximately 1526 to 1867, some 12.5 million slaves had been shipped from Africa, and 10.7 million had arrived in the Americas. The Atlantic Slave Trade was likely the costliest in human life of all of long-distance global migrations.

So, in transit 1.8m died in horrendous conditions and treatment. Then How many were hung in trees, lynched, women and men raped, beaten or worse in actual servitude yet everyone remembers the holocaust and acknowledges the wickedness and horror of that 4year period.

But when it comes to the African 246yr systematic genocide, oppression and abuse it is glossed over told to get over it. Like it was nothing and yet another 100yrs of continuous segregation, miseducation, with yet still to this day No Real Heartfelt Apology for the Treatment of our ancestor and us.

And you have this arrogant yet ignorant so-called president of the free world not only condoning but promoting and enticing the hatred in division in this country by not only looking proud with the chants of send her back. But continuously spouting his own racist comments that feed the flames of the growing division. For those that condone and display such hatred or ignorance shall we go back in time. And recall exactly where you and your ancestor came from having the nerve to yell send her back or tell anyone to go back where they came from. When this so- called great country was built on slavery and deception.

Celebrating thanksgiving where the natives of this land welcomed pilgrims with open arms and taught them how to survive were paid back with treachery and called savages. Yet the savagery that was committed to them was atrocious. But I digress from the point which is the continuous disregard for actual decency and civility in this so-called civilized culture. Where so many think we have come so far yet in these last few years it has been proven how far we still must go. The fact that it's so easily overlooked the disparity and continuous duplicity hidden deep within this American culture.

Could It Be You

Could It be you I have been looking for?
Could it be you who I have seen in my dreams?
Could it be you I have been reaching for with open arms?
Could it be you who leaves me breathless?
Could it be you who has my mind running in circles?
Could it be you who has me in a daze running through a maze?
Could it be you or just a phase?
Could it be you I think of everyday in every way?
Could it be you who I wish to spend the rest of my life with?
Could it be you I choose to be my wife in this life?
Could it be you who brings meaning to my life on this earth?
Could it be you that makes everything seem right day or night?
Could it be you that I love to hold through the night?
Could it be you that I can count on to stand by my side in good and bad times?
Could I be you who deserves my love and my trust when so many others have failed?
Could it be you who appreciates the love I give my heart in hand?
Could it be you who won't play with my heart and do your part to achieve the dreams we have and share?
Could it be you who was meant for me and I for you?

Expressing Myself

So, at every turn you burn one that would be true to only you so as I have tried at every opportunity to express myself and show that there are those few that actually care about you. And in the End, everything you do shows me you are not worthy of a love that is true. Every action causes a reaction so let's take into consideration what has been done.

False accusation, unreal expectations when you commit violations that are subliminal yet atrocious then asking why you can't find one that would love you unconditionally when you had that in your grasp. As I stand apart from any other and far and few in between in a world lacking values and morals. I have given my all in every situation more than needed yet greeted by deceit lies and abuse. There may have been one and only one that myself was not ready and I accept the blame. Yet never cheated, lied or used deception. As I have shouldered the storm through the ups and downs the one that would never hold you down but lift you up when needed. But in return I have been not received the same. When together my eyes would never wander as my focus would always be on you the One, I have chosen to express my inner most feelings, baring my soul with ease to please you and provide you with everything I can. I would never tire of being there holding you close to my heart. Never could I be the one to treat you wrong even when were mad at each other I would never look for another to console me. I would cherish the fact that we are together and be glad that You're at my side through it all. I would try in every way to make you smile understand your position keep communication as key between you and me. I would never play games of the heart or take for granted the trust you placed from our first embrace. Cherishing the bond, we share as we become one till the last breath. As I wonder will I ever find the one that is right for me a love that is meant to be. As this time and place is fallen from grace facing unbelievable odds with so many frauds and fakes in what they claim is the game of life, where love compassion and grace seems to have no place. As I embrace the pain and gain control of my emotions that seem to rise and fall like the crashing of ocean waves. To behave civil amongst those that chose to be sadistic or animalistic is a gift touching the divine with your mind would drive craziest, so I Am thankful I have all my faculties to not be deceived but see through it all as If in a daze. Amazed at his grace even though my body may be broken my soul is outspoken.

Tired Of the Games

As I grow tired of the games and the lies being played. Why is it easy for you to roll the lies of the tip of your lips that drip with sarcasm, envy and jealousy. Refusing to give what you expect to receive to deceive the masses with crossed up classes. Propagating division and mass confusion dividing and conquering trying to keep a hold on power that is slipping through your fingers as light is shown upon the lies. As the veil is being torn asunder and everything done in the dark is in the lights, camera, action the stage being set the curtain drawn back. And I eliminate from my circle those that are untrustworthy unworthy and if alone I must be then so be it. For never truly alone as I put my trust in The Most High and if by chance, I gain an inkling that you are on the wrong side of the track. Even though vengeance is my Eloah, I'm itching to eradicate any snake or evil doer I have been to kind to trusting to passive and that time is over. When you see me give the respect that I give or be ready to receive in kind. As the appreciation for one the actually cares is taken for granted and I have a limit. As I pray each and every day for a better way a way out of this madness surrounding us. As the seasons intermix and you can't tell one from the other the signs of the times that you refuse to adhere or see. Embedded in my soul and mind are the light of Heaven the All Father, The Most High I refuse to burn as I learn to pay head to the laws given for any civilized society. As the world turns 360 degrees on its axis. The questions asked how to be free of this misery how to live this life out of poverty. Many would sow discord and deception while I have a different perception refusing to be deceived by the lies all around me. I have been waiting for this moment it seems for all of my life as I write. And unload to reload and explode make way, cease and desist or I won't resist the urges that permeate my being. Not a threat but a promise for each infraction each infliction whether physically or mentally I have absorbed, deflected to be redirected at the source so as I Aim true don't let it be you in the crosshairs. As I have cared for all my life. I have held back because I know how to act how about you? Can the same be said about you? Even after everything I have been through I still give you the opportunity to fall back before I react. But that time is over as I grow older refusing to let my warm heart grow colder. Letting loose of my anger, my pain that I have maintained for half a century that's been boiling over. Let this be known and written I AM a child of The Most High none other the One True Living Eloah/Elohim/Ahayah all praises to him. Believe what you will you wallow in the swill of a forsaken world because we refuse to follow or listen. So, I return to my ancestry my history not slavery but Hebrew/Israelite/Jew Descendant from Asante/Ashanti. Descendant of Indigenous America's... And Others. As history has been told by the victors but all been a lie. Portraying my color and ancestry as savages yet in truth the most versatile, forgiving and humbling while contributing to every facet of this world as you dig deep into the real history. As I give praise To the Most High you can see it in my eyes and my actions I have turned my cheek week after week year after year upon the slights. The innuendos but no more I have taken enough verbal, physical abuse for a lifetime that time is done and over watch how you act watch how you approach I AM very weary and very tired of the ignorance, the slander, the lies. You have no right, your thinking is in biased upbringing when we have survived 400+ years of ignorance, abuse and miseducation. And I'm grateful to have received such a gift to alleviate my pain and aggression in such a manner. Allowing you the chance to change from the error in your ways. Appreciating the gift given to me as I see ever so clearly watching the signs of the times ignoring the card shuffling games being played to hide ones true agenda. While watching the left and right hands in motion. As the sands of time continue to trickle and the hour glass runs low. This show is not amusing as lives hang in the balance and I refuse to lose focus not falling for the hocus pocus. Life is not a game in a game you have winners and losers I do not play this way. You may think its chess thinking your one or two moves ahead while I AM assessing the bigger picture not a game board. And the using and abusing of each other because of color of skin is not amusing. Instead of ascending we have been descending as I raise my vibration to another level refusing to continue to fall. There is no surprise to the demise in my eyes the pain, the hurt as you skirt on the edge of this cliff. I AM far from perfect and have my own faults but I have always cared and tried to uplift. You have no clue of what I have been through or seen yet you think to demean or scoff. Your loss not mine as I grab hold of the vine life line and hold on for this ride that's coming.

The Age of Enlightenment? A New Beginning?

A New Age Is Dawning

A new age is dawning as I begin to yawn and stretch noticing the opening my eyes and seeing with no surprise what is unfolding. While grabbing a hold and molding my words in such a fashion to begin smashing through the lies that have been wrought over the centuries.

Then to rebuild on a foundation that is solid wielding this pen like a blade forged in heaven given to me by The Most High. This gift that I begin to use not to abuse or amuse but to fuse together this picture.

Raising the banner of The Most High even though coming from a spotted past not letting it consume me with thoughts of vengeance or payback. Watching the mixed reception while wading through the deception as I clean up my own life and my actions staying true to my roots and culture, learning of my heritage and ancestry that was buried under so many fallacies told by the select few that would have you or me lost. But I am finding my way through the lies, Thanking my creator and Christ for being saved and raised to new heights while watching the world through eyes of a different nature. Nurturing the seed planted by our maker being grateful the experiences and lessons I have learned while yearning for more, as I adore this life that is a blessing through the good and bad times accepting my gift and calling to take flight with no fright and fight back against the darkness. That seems to be enveloping our world. Holding back my own feelings of anger or animosity at the atrocities being committed and negate thoughts of greed or lust placing trust in The Most High and his plan. As I'm branded with sevens by his hand forged in heaven sent to this physical existence no fear as my years reach near half a century and I have held back and kept quiet watching no longer while I be silent at the things I have seen or experienced. While praying and being forgiven for my iniquities and changing my thoughts and own actions feeling his presence and power. Watching the hour draw close and the world seemingly not aware or just doesn't care about the dire situation we are facing with the loss of compassion or understanding. So, I thank my creator who is greater for opening my eyes and keeping me safe in these troubled times while I hold my head high and stop wasting time that is precious letting go of wasted emotions to gain control of myself and my own actions.

Actions, Choices and Decisions

Through the pain find peace
Through the sorrow find joy
When life seems unbearable Know you have the power to make a change
With your choices your actions however small have affects you may not see
At the moment but through constant and continuous whether it be dedication
Or persistence being true to yourself and your goals and values will bear fruit when you think no one is watching someone always is
whether to solidify, validate and cement what you portray and display
as your way of thinking and reasons to why you do or act the way that you do. Or to poke holes in and ridicule the things you do.

On My Mind

My mind at any time thoughts a million things a second no time for a quiet place. As we race to a future unknown loving what I am becoming from the lessons given to me by The Most High from the situations he has allowed me to experience and survive to grow from.
The pleasure is mine and I am grateful to know this existence through all the troubles the ups and downs. The time has come to wake up open your eyes look around you what are you doing? Look to the left then the right and finally in the mirror at yourself what is wrong with the picture if anything that you see are you and the ones around you making a difference in a positive light or are you contributing to the negativity affecting this world that we are in together. This day as I take this stance and begin

to make my own moves and opening up. What are you doing with the time you have been given in this existence the gift of knowing physical life as we fight war after war over color or greed instilling fear, hate and animosity as I awaken shaking my head as if in a dream to clear my thoughts before speaking and committing to an action seeing the factions, fractions of humanity in its vanity claiming to be grow yet still children in the grand scheme of things proven by our actions towards each other when we live on this planet together. As I begin to bare the fruit that is planted and take aim at the core problems watching a society that has turned away from the creator from the maker. And we ask why we die or go through what we do when me and you are made in his image yet we commit such atrocious actions towards each other. Expecting respect when giving none. Expecting a hand up when you climb over or pull down another. So, when you look into the mirror what do you see of your own actions instead of pointing at those around you. Who do you surround yourself with? As I begin to remove negativity from my own persona and circle. And I always try to help out when possible but first I must fix and heal myself which I have been doing and by his mercy and grace I am becoming what I am meant to be. Escaping this misery that surrounds us to sound out with my head held high.

Eye Am Growing

This year has been a roller coaster and through it all I have gained so much knowledge not only of myself but of others... and it's been very interesting if you haven't checked out my first almost half century it's been truly eye opening.... it has been recorded all Praises to The Most High. It seems that you truly have no idea no clue as we judge and have been judged.... me myself I may be biased at times I'm not prefect but I do KNOW ONE THING I KNOW NOTHING, But My own experiences and what I have seen others go through. I AM Growing I AM...Knowing More than before.
The sugar coating about to be done.
You want the blue pill continue to sleep and suffer.
You blame God or the Devil when you choose to be wicked over choosing to be good. DO NOT ASK WHY... when you have no respect for yourself or others...Just stop.
This wickedness this deceit. Lies upon Lies...
You can't handle the truth you don't want the truth...
You want a silver spoon.
You want yet do not give.
You want respect yet give none.
You want help yet offer no help.
Just stop it.
Again... what do you offer look in the mirror what change do you give what sacrifice what peace do you offer. You take and give nothing
You want you reach you ask and it is given yet you give nothing Humanity claiming to be grown yet childish behavior and actions...
I myself am far from perfect yet I have given continue to give continue to love and do not complain so no boasting do not presume to judge yet judgement is coming and being

delivered and being dealt out. Be well. I wish you peace. Do not take kindness for weakness. You are being weighed and watched your actions are found wanting I will continue my path I will continue to for myself for you Whether you believe it or don't your choice your decision your gift. free will.
Again, be blessed awaken, or sleep your choice. Peace.

The Façade

As I begin to peel back layer after layer not a player of games when life and emotions are involved, peeping those games being played all around me. Life is not a game or to be taken for granted. As it seems so many think it is and act in such a manner that is demeaning while the meaning of life eludes us to me it is a blessing a physical experience and lesson for the spirit to learn. I have had my own pitfalls, trials and tribulations taking nothing for granted and growing from each situation good and bad. As I begin to stand up and step out taking my time and focusing on the issues at hand yearning to be free of the misery I see around me caused by our own actions or inactions slowly obtaining victory over my own demons and blockades, learning my true ancestry and history not the lies told in a class taught by histories barbaric victors. Seeing history unfold to be told in a different light and I mold these words like clay to say I AM Hebrew. I AM Israelite.
I AM Jewish my ancestry Asanti/Ashanti Tribe of Judah on my fathers' side and my mother Indigenous American Blackfoot as well as European so I AM Blessed to have such a heritage and ancestry as to truly be one with all… and thanking The Most High For this gift of words and rhyme and allowing me this gift of life to experience and record as watcher. And the Sacrifice of his son the Christ to have come to show us how we should treat each other and live. I continuously pray for better days and not just for myself but all of his children and that we wake up and change our ways to grow into what we should and could be. To me the only role model is Christ

worthy of the title King of Kings for his compassion for all. As I rage inside these pages breaking the bonds and chains physically and mentally to be free of humanities constraints that paint a life of woe and agony for our lust, envy and greed and how we treat one another who are one under the Father and Sun on this earth that is truly a paradise we are wasting and squandering. No matter the color, breed nationality needing to pay head to his laws and guidance to actually have a civilized society.

Reality The Brutality Of IT

The Brutality Of this reality that we are living can be unforgiving. But while living and never giving up you can always change your reality for the better. As we proceed to transgress with our aggressions and actions towards each other for none other reason but the color of one skin.To believe one is better because of color I could list so many reasons why my shade makes the grade. But I would be digressing for the point that WE ARE ONE no matter from dark as night to white as snow. Know in the eye of The Most High whose image we are made in your color will not save you from the wickedness you do. The façade one upholds to belittle the next instead of uplifting has me vexed I detest RACISM on any level while uncovering the lies told and sold over generations. I AM tearing the veil aiming at the core of your ignorance in having such a perception propagating the continued deception. Upheld by the few grasping to hold power. As I Awaken and start making it my charge my position to begin, my own inquisition pertaining to the ongoing division lines being drawn sides being taken. Atrocities being committed all over the world. Heralding the oncoming setting for the final confrontation. This direction we are heading by ignoring the warning signs of portent. Instead of progression we regress refusing to cherish each and every life that has no monetary value in other words invaluable. As we refuse cherish this invaluable gift of life taking it for granted. That we step on use, abuse one another to gain physical value yet mental and spiritually we fall. How Long and how far will we fall as humanity the insanity of so called Mankind where actual kindness is far and in between when it should be the norm. My view Respect is given not earned you are given the right to respect by life. Until you give another the reason not to respect you. Then no disrespect is needed but removal from one's circle or dealings.

Pieces of Me

When your mind is fractured into many pieces and it never ceases to amaze you at every venue they mess up the menu I order yet every piece that's shattered is a part of you what do you do you let loose or try to mend and manage each emotion each persona so that you are in control and no other when everything you see is a test at times seeing the ulterior motives of others yet holding back a reaction but recording every action.

To be cataloged and revisited at a later date some would say a grudge yet I say evidence of what not to accept ever again.

To forgive because forgiven yet not forgetting as to not be taken for granted, and at times when it's too much to contain one let's it go pinpointing the action and offense not letting slide that which they do not hide their disgust or disdain when expected to do their job of customer service yet showing every lack thereof. Some claiming respect is earned yet it should be given for what reason must I earn your respect when you give me none. A fallacy a hypocrisy to expect respect that you refuse to show... so as we reap what we sow. And you show every ounce of disrespect and I dissect each action keeping track of actions committed in the moment meant to break me down. As I come around and gather the pieces and let The Most High who is the master Artisan fashion and form my mind into his will and weapon to fight for what is right. To light the way in the darkest hour as we continue to fall from grace. To see the world in the states that it's in and awakened to this madness the sadness I feel at times is overwhelming but I will never be broken again.... weath-

ered the storm through his mercy learned from every life situation to come to this point where I have been given Release from the bottled-up pain. To gain control of almost every aspect of my emotions. Still not fully but close. So thankful for this moment and past that has shown me and allowed me to learn and grow.

Awaken People of the Most High

Awaken My Family
My People from Dark as night to white as snow.
This Life
The Matrix
Yes, the Strength is Within You
The Most High is in you and around you everywhere if you listen and pray attention
YOU ARE BEAUTIFUL
I care have cared for decades yet seems like eons
This World
THE Matrix
Caught between heaven and hell behind the veil.
Whatever You Chose to Call It
YOUR CHOICES MATTER
The Decision you make not only affect you But those around you and more.
What doesn't hurt you may hurt another.
As we enter an age where knowledge is key strokes away.
Some say life is a game in a game you have winners and loser.
My life is not a game. It is not taken lightly.
I win because I choose to grow and learn from my situations and what I see other.

Through the pain find peace

~

Take The Pain And
Through the sorrow find joy
When life seems unbearable and you feel beaten
Know you have the power you are in control
you are a child of The Most High and worthy of
love first and foremost love your creator as you
are made in His image and not a mistake. Love
yourself so you can love others. No matter what
you go through what you deal with you are in
control of your emotions your decisions your
actions are a reflection of who you are as a
person take your pain your sorrow learns from it
and grow do not let it make you bitter. Do not let
it consumes or depress you. Do not let your
emotions control your choices in your head or
outwards you have total control of your choices
and decision. So, with precision I begin to cut
and remove negativity from my surroundings at
times I may react in kind with what you choose
to display but I mostly keep at bay retribution or
reactions of what you display so as I control my

emotions and ambitions to the point of your disrespect that I begin to display my dismay and sorrow for what I am seeing as I awaken to this sadness for choices decision made because of misconceptions

And lies told over centuries when my ancestry dates back to when the Ashanti my heritage my fore fathers represent Hebrew, Jewish and Israelite history. As I research and learn breaking the lies and themental physical chains that have bound and continue to try and bind me no more.. no longer... your lack of respect your disrespect will not be tolerated. As I dissect and rip apart the lies... so as you have broken me shall I break you... into so many pieces until it ceases...

It no longer amazes me what eye am seeing as I awaken to a world lost in chaos... whereeverything is backwards or upside down...... as I turn around and begin to take aim at what eye am seeing and experiencing.... affected by my own choices and others.. and as you amerikkka have torn me to pieces from the inside out so shall it be done to you. You will learn the golden rule treat others how you wish to be treated... so shall I return in kind every jest every fowl gesture. Every purposeful jab, put down, degrading remark and action.
I take analyze and dissect to purposely to not only relieve such pain but refrain from that which is not approved by my father and creator The Most High him whose image I AM Made In and the disrespect the games the lies that have been told. As I dig deeper and research my own

heritage my own lineage and you would claim to be and all I see around me are liar's fakers, facades actor's pretenders and false claims while the flames burn hotter and you perch on the edge of your own demise and I surmise the damage and the perpetrators as you deem to judge and you think your above any other and I watch and record the savagery and misery shall I pin the tail on the donkey. The savagery and blatant hatred is no longer amusing.